Beyond Capitalism

Beyond Capitalism:

New Social Architectures

By

Ladislau Dowbor

Cambridge
Scholars
Publishing

Beyond Capitalism: New Social Architectures

By Ladislau Dowbor

This book first published 2021

Cambridge Scholars Publishing

Lady Stephenson Library, Newcastle upon Tyne, NE6 2PA, UK

British Library Cataloguing in Publication Data
A catalogue record for this book is available from the British Library

ISBN (10): 1-5275-6354-5
ISBN (13): 978-1-5275-6354-4

TABLE OF CONTENTS

PREFACE

We are all in search of new paths. Wolfgang Streeck notes that it may not be the end of capitalism, but it certainly is the end of democratic capitalism. Joseph Stiglitz, on a more optimistic note, suggests we should head towards progressive capitalism; Thomas Piketty, participative socialism. Bernie Sanders recovered the legitimacy and potential of the concept of socialism. But this is not a labeling problem. Solutions are not in the past, despite the strong echo produced by Trump's *Make America Great Again* or Brexit's promise of bringing back sovereignty. Rather, we must understand and qualify the mechanisms behind this sudden hastening of history, the structural transformation of the world we know.

At the time we write, the world witnesses, in awe and fear, as a minute virus spreads its devastating impact, revealing to us all our frailty. After having convinced ourselves that we have been made in the likeness of gods, we realize we are made of the same cells as the rest of nature, smarter for sure, but equally vulnerable. We already consider colonizing Mars, but still need to learn to survive on Earth.

The pandemic striking us did not come alone. Rather, it joins, at a crucial time, a global-scale convergence of critical tendencies. We are a population closing in on 8 billion, rising at 80 million per year, and all wanting to consume more. We are wreaking havoc on the planet's natural environments faster than ever. The disastrous list includes climate change, loss of biodiversity, soil degradation, freshwater pollution, marine pollution from plastic and other residues, resistant bacteria created from antibiotic use on livestock. One needs only a glance at the children living in the dumping grounds surrounding the cities of the world, fighting rats and vultures for garbage, to realize the tragedy.

At another level, and converging with the environmental catastrophe, we have the tragedy of inequality. Cold-blooded statistics show us that 1% of humans hold more accumulated wealth than the other 99%. But these are people, individuals that, rich or poor, white or black, were born with the same potential to contribute to society, a world of possibilities to hope for. A poverty-producing machine criminally sterilizes this potential and reduces these possibilities. Any farmer cultivating the land in Nigeria has more social intelligence and contributes more to humanity than the idiots of Wall Street, who happily shout out that *Greed is Good.*

We have 820 million people starving in the world, out of which 150 million are children, and this, with a daily world production of over 1.5 kilos of food per person. If we divide the world GDP, of about 85 trillion dollars, by the world population, we find that what we now produce could provide three thousand dollars per month per family of four. Our problem is not economic. It lies, rather, in the political and ideological machine that promotes and justifies the absurd partition of the results of human effort, with no connection be it to the most rudimentary merit criterion, or human decency for that matter.

Thus, together with environmental destruction, inequality is a second critical axis. The billions excluded from humanity's achievements, in terms of social progress and technological advances, do not accept this injustice anymore. They feel threatened, unsafe and, in any case, know they are being excluded. They vote, sure enough, on any demagogue preaching hatred against real or imaginary culprits. Hatred has a powerful cathartic effect on frustration. The idea of building a wall between rich and poor, United States and Mexico, – an idea that already failed in the past – shows in a certain way the stark contrast between our technological intelligence and our difficulty to organize a civilized life together. The gap between the political and social sphere is growing. No politics works above a certain level of inequality.

A third critical axis, which will be thoroughly discussed in the present work, is financial chaos. Formerly (that is, a few decades ago), governments issued currency. This was money in the form of paper and coin, which we carried in our pockets, and banks stored in their vaults. Now, 97% of what we modernly call "liquidity" is solely magnetic signals emitted by banks. With governments controlling national spaces and "liquidity" flowing throughout the planet at virtually the speed of light – High-Frequency Trading, as it is now called – there is a radical discrepancy between the financial world and the old regulatory bodies. Global financial chaos has settled in. Its fundamental impact is making financial investments, basically speculation, more profitable and attractive than productive investments.

Money is no longer going where it is needed, particularly to funding the reversion of environmental destruction and the reduction of inequality. Even productive companies are exploited. This has opened the way for fortunes the size of which the world has never seen, in the hands of people who produce nothing. On the contrary, they divert money from the primary function of fostering productive investments and development. Instead, this money is directed to fueling rentism. Joseph Stiglitz, Michael Hudson, Thomas Piketty, Ann Pettifor, and many others have analyzed in detail the notion of rentism. Marjorie Kelly calls this “extractive capitalism”.

The environmental destruction, rising inequality levels, financial chaos, and the present pandemic converge to outline a global systemic crisis. As rarely seen before, numerous researchers and analysts are signaling a structural transformation in terms of how we organize ourselves on this small celestial object called Earth. I have no doubt we are dealing with a crisis of civilization.

The converging crises open up an immense space for new ideas. The extensive alterations in political culture create opportunities for change. But to establish and play by the new rules, we must delve into the current mechanisms and understand how the forces are structured, as well as the viable alternatives. The future is not written. The four crises interact chaotically. However, the last link, the minute virus that paralyzed the planet, has, precisely by forcing a halt in activities, opened space for change. We may, of course, overcome the virus and go back to slowly destroying the planet. But the chaos generated holds an immense opportunity for change. We can in fact think beyond capitalism.

INTRODUCTION

The technology has such potential that its impact on society is widely expected to be as profound as the industrial revolution.
—New Scientist, April 23, 2018

Prosperity for all cannot be delivered by austerity-minded politicians, rent-seeking corporations and speculative bankers. What is urgently needed now is a global new deal.
—Unctad. 2017, ii

World history is nothing but an endless, dreary account of the rape of the weak by the strong…The externals of civilization – technology, industry, commerce and so on – also require a common basis of intellectual honesty and morality.
—Hermann Hesse, The Glass Bead Game, 1943

A working hypothesis may prove very useful. We propose here to consider a set of transformations currently underway through the concept of change in the mode of production. Capitalism is changing. According to the analytical framework, we find developments on different notions, such as the informational factor in productivity and the network society (Manuel Castells), the advent of the "immaterial" (André Gorz), the zero marginal cost society (Jeremy Rifkin), the sharing economy (Arun Sundararajan), financial capitalism (François Chesnais, David Harvey), global capitalism (Joseph Stiglitz), the complexity era (Edgard Morin), parasitic capitalism (Zygmunt Bauman), and the world-systems (Immanuel Wallerstein). Alvin Toffler, in *The Third Wave*, already signaled the search for an integrated approach. We all strive to make sense of modernity as it advances. There is no global previous "scheme", but there will be, beyond any doubt, a systemic resultant arising from the convergence of present chaotic processes of transformation. A whole different animal is being born.

Capitalism is changing rapidly and deeply. Certain labels are used to characterize its changes or order its stages. We have imperialist, liberal, rentier, and also neoliberal or global, dependent or dominant, central or peripheral capitalism. We may yet refer to a set of rules, like those of the Washington Consensus, to present a more integrated view of what we mean to express, or refer to the 3rd and 4th industrial revolutions, or even to the Anthropocene. In general terms, we refer to "all of that" as neoliberalism.

The animal is still the same, but with different colors, a larger mane, a more or less aggressive behavior, with more or less cohesive parts. In epistemological terms, we end up saving ourselves by adding "neo" or "post" to different scientific schools of thought.

As changes become more pronounced, however, and the more traditional concepts no longer adequately describe the real world, we are naturally led to wonder whether we are still studying variations of the same animal, or characteristics of a new, yet to be born one. The butterfly is a transformation of the chrysalis, but it is radically different. This approach presents no impediments; scientific orthodoxy has already assimilated the view that the sum of quantitative changes leads to a qualitative mutation. In the present study, we will discuss a set of changes in capitalism that may characterize the evolution towards another mode of production, which can be described as informational, constituting another era different from the industrial one: the era of knowledge.

Although adding labels to the traditional image of capitalism may help, it may prove more instructive to adopt a hypothesis of transition into a new mode of production, in which the different vectors of change in society together form another systemic logic. This new logic characterizes another mode of production. This approach seems to me more useful than the idea of another matrix or paradigm. My question is whether it would be more productive, in scientific terms, to use the framework of industrial capitalism and note how the past is deforming or to look towards the future and consider what new system is emerging.

From the industrial revolution, we inherited machine-based production relations, the private property of the means of production, the relation between the bourgeoisie and proletariat, and profit and salary. What are the trends and new relations brought about by this new era, marked by a revolution in knowledge, rapid advances in communication and information technologies, and the rise of immaterial money? What are the new inner workings? Which are the novel exclusions? We will not attempt to answer such broad questions, but rather understand how changes may gain clarity and understandability when submitted to analysis as parts of a new dynamics and not alterations of an old one. The idea of a 4.0 Industrial Revolution frankly does not help. I am convinced that it is much more than that. The technological revolution we are currently witnessing is much more than a stage of the Industrial Revolution.

We will approach the matter as a broader social transformation, broad enough to generate a knowledge society, just as we have had agrarian and industrial societies. In this perspective, there are massive implications. The many agrarian societies of the past had political structures and production relations established around a key factor: the land. The industrial society had political structures and production relations based on the private property of the new means of production: machines. What political structure and production relations will organize the societies in which the key factor is knowledge?

In the land era, the feud, or fence, was the boundary. The property was based on family relations and connected to nobility. Production relations were based on slavery or serfdom. Minds were controlled through religion and by the corresponding ecclesiastical power. In the industrial era, walls and gateways were placed around factories, the property was based on control over the means of production, and production relations were based on workers' wages and the surplus-value. Minds were controlled through consumerism and advertising. Is there a similar systemic order for the era of knowledge and technological revolution?

Marx's views, his approach to macro-social analysis, remain stubbornly relevant. It is essential, however, to reconstruct the concepts, rather than simply transpose them. While analyzing the industrial revolution, Marx did the work of showing the new technical relations of production (the division of labor, socialization of production, the birth of the factory environment); the resulting social relations (based on wages and the surplus-value in particular); and the new power relations (based on the private property of the means of production). This infrastructure corresponded to certain superstructures, characteristic of capitalism: the bourgeois democracy and the legal system, as well as the elements that form a corresponding value system: the liberal ideology, the *homo economicus*, and the money and consumption culture. Furthermore, the system's legitimacy was associated with the fair remuneration of capital (profit) and work (salary). Each system's narrative is also fundamental.

With this pair – infrastructure and superstructure – Marx characterized the capitalist mode of production. With the new technical and social relations, and new forms of power and surplus appropriation, can we still use the same frame of reference? Labor exploitation not only continues but worsens, as the data on inequality indicate. Exploitation is, however, common to all systems and may repeat itself within renewed dynamics and mechanisms. The question may be premature, given the novelty of the trends, but it is legitimate. The answer will probably depend on the ability of the new global elites – new, since they essentially manipulate symbols and images and are now scarcely found in factory management – to absorb the emerging dynamics to their advantage.

The new society undeniably brings with it both a potential for liberation and the grim prospect of an oppressive future, to the likes of Orwell's *1984* or Huxley's *Brave New World*. Yet, if the outcome is grim, the new forms of domination will not necessarily characterize a capitalist mode of production. When social surplus appropriation ceases to happen primarily through salary exploitation, the changes are qualitative. The systemic logic behind the processes of social reproduction is thus rearranged and shifted. Bill Gates or Carlos Slim's billionaire appropriations are set upon immaterial systems and not factories. David Harvey, in *The Madness of Economic Reason*, rightly notes that Thomas Piketty's "capital", in *Capital of the 21st Century*, is not precisely capital, but wealth. It is in any case worthwhile listing, orderly, the great axes of change, the mega-trends that are generating a new world. New does not mean better: environmental, social, and economic issues are critically worsening. But, without a doubt, things are functioning differently.

I –

THE TRANSFORMATION IN THE PRODUCTIVE BASIS OF SOCIETY

Capitalism emerges as a revolution in the productive forces: by connecting machines to new energy sources, we began operating machines with an external energy supply. Now, we program machines. We generate primarily knowledge, technology, design, all of which are immaterial. This is not restricted to the field of robotics, which increasingly penetrates different industries. The local farmer now uses artificial insemination and soil analysis, and physicians have the support of laboratory networks and perform remote surgeries. The central axis of change is that technology is now the main factor of production. This modifies capitalism, since technological knowledge, different from machines and physical labor, is immaterial. Machines are still important, for sure, but incorporated knowledge is the structuring axis. Knowledge is an immaterial asset.

Technology as the main factor of production

Jeremy Rifkin's studies about the zero marginal-cost society help to size the ongoing transformation. Physical goods – watches, for example – are rivalrous, because if someone takes them, another person ceases to have them. This is why private property is central in the capitalist society. But if I share knowledge, I will not be deprived of it; knowledge is a non-rivalrous good. This means that in the modern economy, the supply of the main factor of production is not affected by use. On the contrary, it can be multiplied indefinitely. This opens new epistemological grounds for economics, a science that is based on optimizing the allocation of scarce resources. The main factor of production is not scarce. This also explains why so many corporations strive to produce artificial scarcity to charge access. The nature of a factor that can be multiplied indefinitely without additional cost is, precisely, open access. Restricting access to good ideas makes no sense; it is dramatic underuse of a potential tool for society's development. We have moved historically from the land to machines and from machines to knowledge. The productive basis of society is shifting radically and quickly, with profound impacts on the entire system's logic.

The revolution in the system of knowledge expansion

There is no denying that the information era has transformed our mode of production. We have innovative scientific applications in almost every sector: energy, transportation, medicine, education, culture, new materials, and so on. However, the depth and rhythm of innovation highly depend on the capacity of expanding and managing knowledge. Alan Turing's conceptual developments and subsequent decoding machine changed the face of World War II and brought us a knowledge machine, marking the start of the digital age. The ability to express virtually all units of information, whether letters, numbers, colors or sounds, with only two signals, "0" and "1", made it possible to embed human knowledge in magnetic signals. This is a radical innovation in the innovative capacity itself: the machine's machine, the brain's extension. Knowledge, since then, progressively dismisses the physical mediums – books, paintings, discs – to which it was previously tied. The main factor of production, an intangible one, encounters its immaterial medium, the magnetic signal.

It is hard to picture research on DNA, for instance, without computers. It is especially hard to imagine innovation in computing power without computing itself. In 1776, while considering the mechanization of pin production, Adam Smith foresaw a massive transformation, which led him to outline the characteristics of the industrial revolution. His work is to date relevant. Rather than the quantitative aspect of manufacturing (insignificant at the time), he focuses on its potential to transform society as a whole. Just as the evolution of looms led to improved weaving techniques, the economy of knowledge now improves the tool for managing knowledge: computing. In this way, transformations undergo a cumulative and interactive process. Our evolution into a society of knowledge and the fact that we have the corresponding tools indicate a transformation as profound as that of the industrial revolution. The machine of today is, in a way, the knowledge machine. Knowledge, as the new basis of the economy, has produced its own corresponding "machine". It is radically different for being, essentially, immaterial. We are facing the digital revolution.

Knowledge and connectivity: the internet era

In terms of a historical process of transformation, we are still at the beginning. Two billion people still cook with firewood, and more than one billion still have no access to electricity. But widespread digital inclusion is only a matter of years now, as it is not just in the interest of the excluded, but also of various agents in the process. The era of knowledge is rapidly spreading computers across the households of the world where there is reasonable income. It is on its way to reaching every company and government department, every airplane, car, and pocket. It is not just one more technology. It is what enables receiving, storing, handling, and interconnecting nearly unlimited amounts of knowledge. This technology is triggering a cumulative process of expansion.

The industrial capitalist economy set up production and distribution infrastructures, covering the planet with power grids, railroads, highways, and telecommunication networks, as well as other systems that organize productive processes. The era of knowledge has surpassed telegraphy and good old telephony to generate global connectivity. Since we are experiencing transformations from the inside, so to speak, we may sometimes fail to realize the earthshaking impact of the fact that we can now instantly connect to any person or company, and even a document, movie or information unit, in any part of the world, at practically no cost. This is the agea of total and global connectivity, an immaterial universe that works at practically the speed of light. Contrary to the audacious assumption of the *end of history*, we are witnessing faster and deeper transformations than ever before. We have a dominant factor of production that is immaterial (knowledge), the means for storing and handling it (computing), and the global connectivity necessary to make this factor of production instantly available at any given place, to any given person. This, in terms of economic, social, and political organization, is much more than a stage in industrial capitalism.

Redefining space and territory

In the era of "Space is Dead" and "The World is Flat", of everything-here-and-now, the very concepts of territory, belonging, and identity are changing. People create social bonds according to a variety of interests; productive processes are internationally coordinated; financial flows cross the planet instantly; new forms of economic, social and cultural organizations are starting to form and with them, of course, new forms of political organization, in which the roles of national spaces are being redefined, and significantly weakened.

The idea of imperialism as a superior stage of capitalism is familiar. We are moving beyond this view. The so-called Third World, distant and unknown until a few centuries ago, was first enslaved, then colonized (when the peoples had the privilege of being enslaved in their own land) and, more recently, in the context of industrial imperialism, exploited by the industrialized countries. The Third World countries now strive to find space within the narrow range of possibilities opened to them by the dominant economies. They have achieved independence and supposedly sovereignty. But they are tied to a planetary machine of economic and financial power that increasingly articulates political and cultural power as well. How will the space of the 20th-century Nation-states be redefined in the globalized world of the 21st century?

Corporations, which are central political and economic agents of the new globalization, are organized in networks across the planet. Each one of them covers dozens or even up to a hundred countries, influencing or controlling politics, justice, the media, and culture. This is not new. The same tendency is described in Marx and Engels' 1848 Manifesto. Once more, however, accumulated quantitative changes have led to a qualitative systemic change. The nationalist clamors, present in Trump's *Make America Great Again* or the UK's Brexit, seem like the dying cry of the past century's glories. For better or worse, a new world is forming. When will we acknowledge that virtually all large corporations use tax havens, a type of financial extraterritoriality ("off-shore" is a meaningful notion), to manage their financial assets beyond the reach, as well as the knowledge, of governments?

We must, as a set of national economies with foreign trade, move beyond capitalism to analyze its process of worldwide osmosis. There is a systemic discrepancy between the global dimension of the economy and the fragmented regulatory power of the nations. The scores of companies that constituted the entrepreneurial world of the past needed a regulatory State to guarantee order and respect to contracts. With the reorganized world of corporations, politics is being rescaled and played by corporations themselves. A whole new animal is being born. In terms of the mode of production, the changes in infrastructure are generating new superstructures, as we will later see.

The intangible economy

We are rapidly becoming a global society, demographically established in cities, and with a knowledge-based economy – what André Gorz calls the *immaterial* and others call the *intangible*. In *Capitalism without Capital*, Haskel and Estaque note that, at the turn of the millennium, there was an inversion in the proportion of investments in physical equipment in comparison to the investments in technology, design, image, and the like – the intangibles. The main investment flows do not result in machines or chimneys anymore, but in a broader capacity to control organized knowledge. In the last century, the capitalist was, and will surely continue to be during a large part of this century, the factory and harvest owner. However, the present-day capitalist is increasingly becoming the controller of immaterial assets, such as virtual platforms, apps, patents, and copyrights. They also control financial flows: magnetic signals that define other equally immaterial – and drastically more powerful – forms of appropriation and control.

It is worthwhile to examine the great fortunes of the new economic world: among them, there are no factories or machines, but instead technology, software, virtual intermediation platforms, organization systems, algorithms, and artificial intelligence. We notice that a fundamental theoretical shift is necessary to understand these new processes: we are not dealing with the ownership of the means of production but of the control systems. Will the concept of the socialization of the means of production remain the same? It is also equally important to remember that the first in-depth analysis of the world corporate system, conducted in 2011 by the Swiss Federal Institute of Technology (ETH Zurich), is called *The Network of Global Corporate Control*. The idea of such a network goes much further than the concept of property. The authors even estimated that the concentration of power through control was ten times larger than what the companies' valuation showed at first glance. The concept of the private property of the means of production has changed. Bloomberg's list of the largest fortunes is highly informative:

Bloomberg ▸ Bloomberg Billionaires Index

Rank	Name	Total net worth ▾	$ Last change	$ YTD change	Country	Industry
1	Jeff Bezos	**$100B**	+$328M	+$35.0B	United States	Technology
2	Bill Gates	**$91.7B**	+$154M	+$9.33B	United States	Technology
3	Warren Buffett	**$85.8B**	+$311M	+$12.6B	United States	Diversified
4	Amancio Ortega	**$75.2B**	-$491M	+$3.10B	Spain	Retail
5	Mark Zuckerberg	**$73.4B**	+$119M	+$23.4B	United States	Technology
6	Bernard Arnault	**$63.3B**	-$334M	+$24.1B	France	Consumer
7	Carlos Slim	**$62.7B**	+$402M	+$12.9B	Mexico	Diversified
8	Larry Ellison	**$53.3B**	+$152M	+$11.7B	United States	Technology
9	Larry Page	**$52.5B**	-$84.6M	+$12.6B	United States	Technology
10	Ingvar Kamprad	**$52.4B**	-$3.92M	+$8.41B	Sweden	Retail

Source: https://www.bloomberg.com/billionaires/

If a traditional 20th-century company went bankrupt, creditors could sell the machines and equipment and recover a large part of the money. In the case of the fortunes above, if the corresponding companies went bankrupt, they would yield only wishful thinking and a bad reputation. The concept of the value of the means of production has changed, and so has the way social surplus is extracted and transformed into wealth.

Haskel and Westlake dedicate a good part of their book, *Capitalism without Capital*, to capturing the profound differences that characterize the intangible capital. It is different from

> a physical asset like a factory or a shop or a telephone line: once these assets reach their capacity, you need to invest in new ones. But intangibles do not have to obey the same set of physical laws: they can generally be used again and again. Let's call this characteristic of intangibles scalability... It should come as no surprise that things that one can't touch, like ideas, commercial relationships, and know-how, are fundamentally different from physical things like machines and buildings. (60-61)

This is an earthshaking transformation. Intangible assets, being indefinitely reproducible, open the way for a global, widespread increase in productivity without additional costs. These are not studies on the possible outcomes: while comparing the dynamics of the added value in the manufacturing and services sectors in the United States and France, the authors noticed an inversion in the relative importance of tangible and intangible assets.

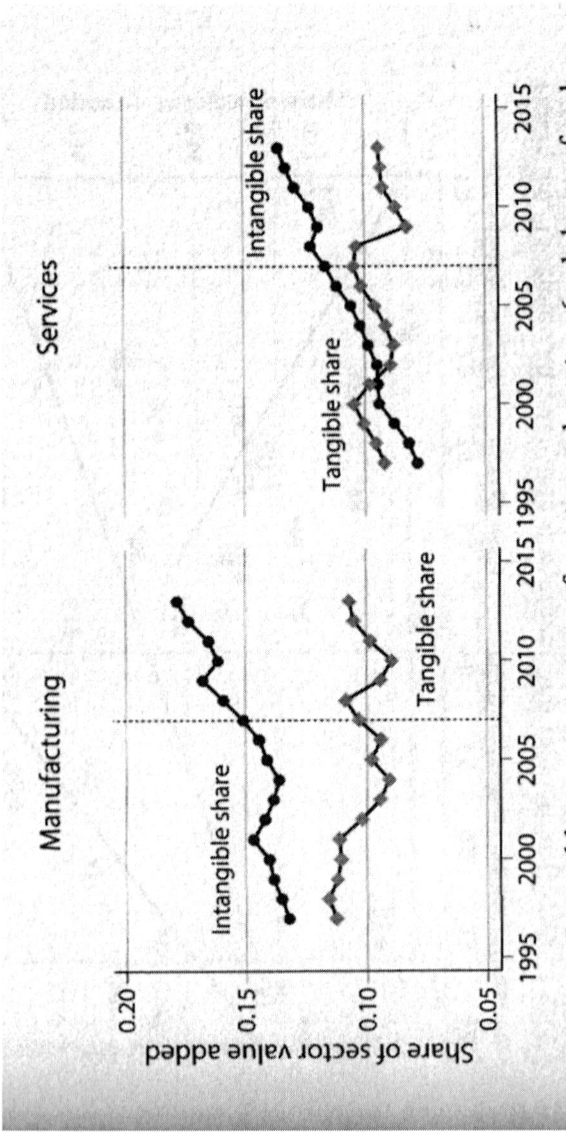

Figure 2.7. Intangible intensity in manufacturing and services (real shares of real sector value added, EU and US, non-farm business). Source: authors' calculations from INTAN-Invest (www.intan-invest.net) and SPINTAN (www.spintan.net) databases.

Source: Haskel and Westlake, *Capitalism without Capital,* 31

Naturally, intangible goods do not simply substitute tangible ones. We still need food, housing, transportation, and such, but in essence, the actual physical costs, like those of raw materials and traditional labor – the stevedore's back, so to speak – become, in due proportion, increasingly secondary in the productive processes. Furthermore, those who control the intangible assets also progressively control the traditional productive systems. In the knowledge era, in which new technological processes and new forms of taking over the surplus and the political systems are gaining prominence, agriculture and manufacturing will not be substituted but subjected to a new logic that must be clarified.

The guideline of Haskel and Westlake's research:

> Our central argument in this book is that there is something fundamentally different about intangible investment, and that understanding the steady move to intangible investment helps us understand some of the key issues facing us today: innovation and growth, inequality, the role of management, and financial and policy reform. We shall argue there are two big differences with intangible assets. First, most measurement conventions ignore them. There are some good reasons for this, but as intangibles have become more important, it means we are now trying to measure capitalism without counting all the capital. Second, the basic economic properties of intangibles make an intangible-rich economy behave differently from a tangible-rich one. (7)

In the present study, this is precisely what we focus on: to what extent do the changes in "basic economic properties" change not only the economy but the mode of production, in the broader sense?

An indefinitely multipliable wealth

Let us return to Jeremy Rifkin. The concept that names his book, the *zero marginal-cost society*, may seem foreign to non-economists, but the principle is very simple: as we penetrate the society of knowledge and the creative economy, the axis for economic analysis changes. We enter the immaterial economy, as André Gorz calls it. In it, the main factor of production, knowledge, may be spread across the world once it is produced, with free, unlimited access, and zero additional cost. If I pass on a physical good to someone, I cease to have it. It is said to be a "rival good", and having its ownership is essential. But if I pass on an idea, I will still have it; it is a "non-rival good". The rational allocation of scarce supplies is the traditional object of economics. In this new context, the entire framework for economic analysis based on scarcity has shifted. Instead of increasing production to increase profit, capitalism starts searching for ways to create artificial scarcity and to combat decentralized, collaborative processes of wealth multiplication.

The system thus produces a value inversion. Denying free access to the books and movies you could find online becomes central to the dominant system. To the consumer, however, easy access is what matters. After the initial costs of production are covered, and a reasonable profit is made, is there any excuse for charging each additional access that generates no cost? After all, do the rules that apply to an economy of goods, in which new investments are required for every new unit produced, apply to goods and services that may be infinitely reproduced at zero cost?

How do we organize an economy, Rifkin asks,

> where the marginal costs of generating, storing, and sharing communications, energy, and a growing number of products and services are heading to nearly zero? A new communication/energy matrix is emerging, and with it a new "smart" public infrastructure. The Internet of Things (IoT) will connect everyone and everything in a new economic paradigm that is far more complex than the First and Second Industrial Revolutions, but one whose architecture is distributed rather than centralized. Even more important, the new economy will optimize the general welfare by way of laterally integrated networks on the Collaborative Commons, rather than vertically integrated businesses in the capitalist market. (56)

Rifkin coherently provides open access to his book, which is in itself an example of the transformation. Through the book, he is disseminating knowledge about economic mechanisms, contributing to society's educational level and, on a small scale, also to productivity and general well-being. Prosperity is a social construction. Is the author forgoing profit? It turns out he is actually amplifying his reach. The invitations he will consequently receive to expose his ideas will earn him more money and, probably, he will sell yet more books in the traditional format. In this knowledge-dense, immaterial economic cycle, we must balance paid and collaborative tasks, aware that as knowledge becomes the main factor of production, the indirect profit dimension broadens. These are the new forms of balance being established.

This is not restricted to sharing music with friends or uploading videos on YouTube. Rifkin provides several examples in finance, where numerous peer-to-peer (P2P) networks enable financial flows between those who have stagnant resources and those who need them, dodging the abusive interest rates and tariffs charged by financial intermediaries. With the rapidly decreasing costs of photovoltaic cells, independent energy production rapidly grows in households, as well as networks for transferring the surplus energy. In the logistics sector, trucks traditionally perform a significant amount of empty travels. The creation of an information network on current truck loads and destinations allows companies to transport each other's loads, optimizing routing plans and reducing fuel costs. Individual truck owners will also belong to an information network in which knowledge of the flows can improve logistics as a whole, letting them make decisions without having to wait for orders. These are the so-called organizational benefits; they are highly productive, even if immaterial. Loss reduction and process improvement may even result in a GDP reduction. They do, however, certainly improve our economies' performances. My online communication improves my productivity, but the fact that I do not use the traditional mail services reduces employment and transportation costs that would be accounted for as economic activity, GDP growth.

Advertisement is also changing. Instead of buying because the ad says the product is wonderful, customers now read the barcode with their phones and a list of previous buyers' opinions appear on the screen – filtered to cut out the false personal opinions that companies try to include. As the audiences migrated from the television to the internet, especially the younger generations, so did advertisements. This was not easy, however. People were used to commercial breaks on television, but advertisement interruption on the internet makes people annoyed and produces negative brand perception. Times are changing. The common ground is that the new global connectivity and the dominant immaterial dimension of the main factor of production are demanding new rules to the game.

To Rifkin, the rapid expansion of this new economy opens the possibility to escape the giants of intermediation and shows a way out of an economic dog-eat-dog mentality. The way is progressively opening for direct collaboration between economic agents, who are now at the same time producers and consumers, the well-known "prosumers". Is this excessive optimism? Perhaps. But instead of knowledge on how favorable the future will be, we take from the book a good understanding of the rising opportunities for a more humane economy.

Haskel and Westlake summarize the essential aspect of the intangible economy, of being indefinitely expandable with little or no additional costs, through the concept of scalability:

> From an economic point of view, scalability derives from a key feature of ideas: what economists call 'non-rivalry.' If I drink a glass of water, you cannot drink the same glass: it is a 'rival' good. But if I use an idea, you too can use the same idea: the idea is non-rival. (...) This scalability applies to many sorts of intangible assets. Once a business has created or acquired an intangible asset, it can usually make use of it again and again at relatively little cost, compared to most physical assets. (66/65)

When saline solution was found to provide oral rehydration, its use spread across the world, saving millions of children, and no one thought of issuing a patent and restricting access to its benefits. The widespread use of this technology did not harm its creator. But could money be made from a patent in this case? We are at the heart of a set of new dilemmas related to economic organization. Is a person or company's possible profit more important than the potential social benefit? The contradiction between the social process of production and the private appropriation of the results becomes particularly evident. Gar Alperovitz and Lew Daly studied this subject in their book *Unjust Deserts*, as we will later see.

Haskel and Westlake, with no Marxism, summarize the tendency clearly: "The social rate of return exceeds the private rate" (112). The obstacles presented by bureaucracy, patents, and copyrights lead to less profit at the individual level in comparison to the potential social benefits of open access. In terms of systemic productivity, private appropriation may become increasingly unproductive. The balance between individual benefits and social interests is changing. Let us not forget that today, a new segment of intermediaries has specialized in buying patents to later charge fees from companies who wish to produce further research or develop products. Between the innovator's stimulus to earn profit and society's diffuse interests, we must consider the general concept of remuneration for intangible goods. The authors quote Thomas Jefferson: "He who receives an idea from me receives instruction himself without lessening mine; as he who lights his taper at mine, receives light without darkening me" (72).

***

The huge transformation of the dominant productive processes is undeniable. We are witnessing a technology boom. We are gaining progressive control over the very process of knowledge expansion. And the supply of this factor of production is not affected by use. Furthermore, with global connectivity, intelligent connections between information, documents, people, and institutions can be made with virtually no additional costs. The traditional spaces that circumscribed the realm of specific economic activities are being dismantled. The traditional farming or manufacturing units are now controlled by financial or informational systems with platforms, networks, and algorithms. The newly established technical relations of production transform the productive processes, which in turn deeply transform the social relations of production. During feudalism, the main factor of production was the land; during industrial capitalism, it was the machine. Now it is knowledge, which, as a factor of production, requires different institutions. From the feudal lord and serf to the industrial capitalist and factory worker, the social relations of production change. What will come along with the new horizons?

II –

THE CHANGES IN THE SOCIAL RELATIONS OF PRODUCTION

We saw above the massive changes in the content of productive processes. Naturally, we will continue producing wheat and rice, steel and automobiles. But the basic element of value formation, the main factor of production, is a set of intangible activities that may be generalized without significant additional costs. When manufacturing first appeared, agriculture did not vanish. On the contrary, it had to be intensified to provide food for the cities and raw materials for the factories. But the dominant axis of the social structure became manufacturing, which in turn transformed agriculture itself. With the emergence of knowledge and intangibles in general, manufacturing and agriculture gained productive capacity. This is due precisely to the advances in the intangible activities that now dominate transformations. But those who have control are not necessarily the same as those who control machines anymore.

Just as the logic of industrial accumulation dominated social relations of production during the late 19th century and the 20th century, today, the dynamics that structure society are access to information and control over knowledge, in a broad sense. André Gorz summarizes, in the very first pages of his study *The Immaterial*, the extent of the transformations:

> The wide acceptance of knowledge as the main productive force caused a change that compromises the validity of the key economic categories and indicates the need to establish another economy. The knowledge economy that is currently spreading is a form of capitalism that aims to redefine its main categories – labor, value, and capital – and in this way embraces new domains. (9)

Controlling knowledge is controlling society's main factor of production. Ignacy Sachs synthesized this idea very well: over the last century, power was in the hands of factory controllers. In this century, power will be in the hands of those who control information. Just as the logic of social organization changed with the transition from the agrarian to the industrial era, so will we face a profound systemic change with the information era. This framework seems to us more informative of the fast-paced changes we are living through than the idea of a fourth industrial revolution. The technical bases of the productive processes have changed. We will see the impacts of this on the social relations of production as a whole.

From market competition to intercompany organization

In the manufacturing world, the tendency to grow to monumental proportions has always been strong. The possibility of spreading the fixed costs of machines and equipment over more products generally guaranteed the so-called economies of scale. General Motors is an emblematic case, among many others. This is the logic of large production companies with specific products: when we speak of GM cars, we know who and what we are talking about. The business giants below own assets larger than the GDP of most countries. They have also created networks in which they have shareholding control over various activities. Warren Buffett's Berkshire Hathaway, ranking seventh in the list below, was initially in the textile sector but is now essentially a financial holding company. It controls and extracts dividends from different businesses, in rail transportation, encyclopedias, media, vacuum cleaners, jewelry, electricity, natural gas, and in particular insurance. It shares interests with Goldman Sachs and Bill Gates is its second-largest shareholder. It all stays in the family. Alphabet controls Google, and Tencent is a Chinese tech and video game giant.

Market value, in million dollars – 2018

(Current Market Cap)	Short Name	Market Cap
1	APPLE INC	860.88B
2	ALPHABET INC-A	729.29B
3	MICROSOFT CORP	659.91B
4	AMAZON.COM INC	563.54B
5	FACEBOOK INC-A	514.99B
6	TENCENT	493.56B
7	BERKSHIRE HATH-A	489.25B
8	ALIBABA GRP-ADR	441.62B
9	JOHNSON&JOHNSON	375.36B
10	JPMORGAN CHASE	371.05B

Source: https://www.theguardian.com/business/2018/jan/03/apple-leads-race-to-become-world-first-1tn-dollar-company

The economic weight of these groups is highlighted by The Guardian:

> The world's top five companies are collectively worth $3.35tn – more than the gross domestic product of the UK and every other country on Earth bar the US, China, Japan and Germany. The huge increase in valuations came after global stock markets ended 2017 at record highs, as share prices benefitted from President Donald Trump's tax cuts and continued quantitative easing from central banks.

They are giants, but giants whose massive bodies are essentially the control networks that allow them to extract dividends. If their machines and facilities were to be sold, they would not yield much. Their value is fundamentally immaterial and lies in their systemic ability to extract dividends. The occasional factory is merely an outsourced provider under their control. Interests are arranged in an entirely different way in comparison to the traditional entrepreneurial system. These corporations' valuations are based on their stock price, which in turn depends on the dividends paid to shareholders. At the top of the pyramid, we find the assets of the new economy, which are essentially immaterial. What material support would be sold with Facebook?

The transformation was followed by a curious shift in the concept of the market. As defined in classical economic theory, the concept referred to the free exchange of goods and services, leading to a natural balance between prices and quantities. Since there are numerous companies, none can dominate and distort the process. This type of market still exists, for example, in the t-shirt industry and other similar ones. In these cases, the consumer population may be “free to choose”, as Milton Friedman would say. Today, when we refer to the market, what comes to mind is a group of large financial intermediaries supervising the rates of return on equity and other financial investments.

Tencent, the Chinese-based multinational figuring right after Facebook in the table above, provides a good idea of a modern corporation. In a simple Wikipedia query, we learn that this group controls e-commerce activities, video gaming, software, virtual reality, ride-sharing, banking, financial services, fintech, consumer technology, computer technology, automobiles, film production, movie ticketing, music production, space technology, natural resources, smartphones, big data, agriculture, medical services, cloud computing, social media, e-books, internet services, education, renewable energy, artificial intelligence, robotics, food delivery, and others. Any sector, any country, in joint business partnerships with various companies, from YouTube to L’Oréal. You have probably never heard of Tencent and, nonetheless, you have surely engaged in purchases that feed this company’s controllers. A part of your money goes into their pockets.[1]

[1] Guardian, 13 Jan. 2018 – “Tencent is one of three Chinese internet behemoths, including Baidu and Alibaba, known collectively as BAT. China’s answer to Silicon Valley’s power club known as the FANGs – Facebook, Amazon, Netflix and Google.” https://www.theguardian.com/business/2018/jan/13/tencent-the-500bn-chinese-tech-firm-you-may-never-have-heard-of.

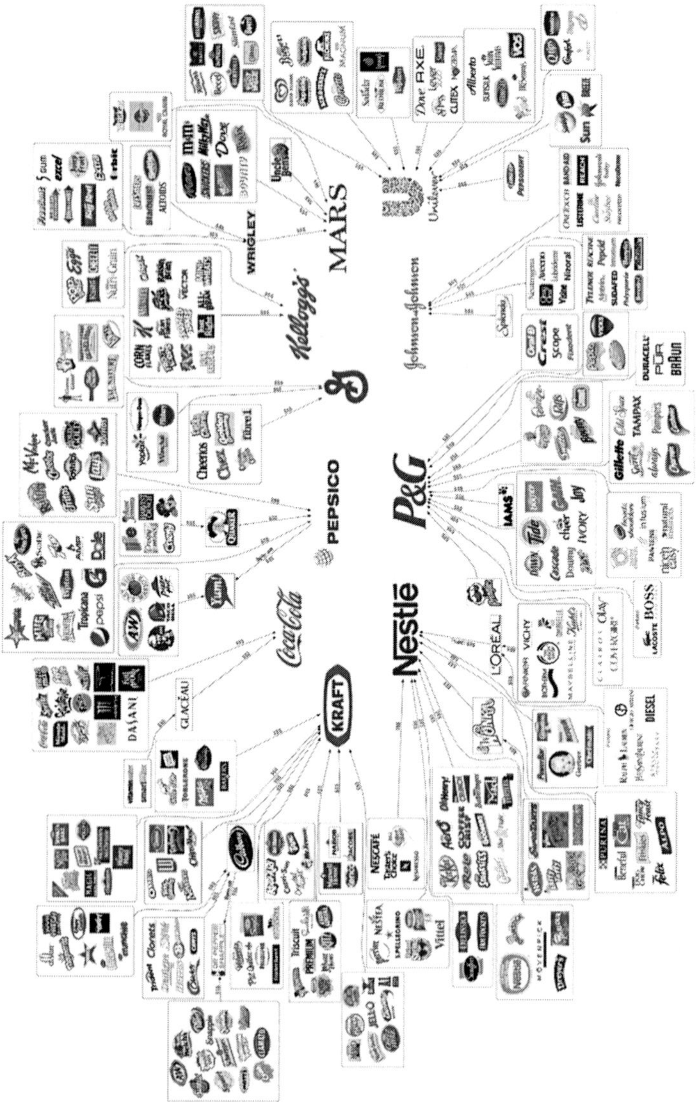

Source: http://www.huffingtonpost.com/2012/04/27/consumer-brands-owned-ten-companies-graphic_n_1458812.html

The world has radically changed and is changing even more, at a fast pace. We are familiar with the end products that show up in supermarket aisles, but information on who owns these products, who controls them, and which environmental, social, or even consumer security policies they adopt is clearly beyond our reach. The groups above are financial holdings that control other financial institutions across different sectors and countries which, in turn, control companies that effectively produce things we consume. Names such as Nestlé are kept only due to the decades of investments spent to associate the brand with positive images. At the top are financial managers that understand very little of the productive spheres. Not that they could anyway, considering the myriad of products, sectors, and countries where they operate. From a free-market world, we passed to gigantic pyramids of financial power, organized in complex systems of interrelations. In the absence of a system of global political governance, the global economic system is creating its own network of power. In the excellent saying that Octávio Ianni left us, *politics moved to a different place.*

From production profits to financial investment income

In another study, *The Age of Unproductive Capital*, we presented a study by the Swiss Federal Institute for Technological Research showing that today, 737 groups control 80% of the corporate world, out of which 147 control 40%, and two-thirds of these are banks.[2] The systemic logic radically changes, because these groups' major interest is their financial returns, which are determined by those at the top of the pyramid. Entrepreneurial decisions are traditionally made by producers of concrete goods or services, whose interests include providing quality services to customers. The decision-making environment is now changing. The profound change in terms of who sits in the controlling position leads to a shift in the extraction of the surplus from the productive processes. The controlling shareholders, or different types of financial controllers, see the production company at the base of the pyramid as a unit of dividend extraction. A company unit that produces goods or services could have structural and long-term policies for community insertion, employer educational assistance, and investment in local sustainable development. To Billiton or Bradesco's shareholders (the latter through Vale or Vale-Par), maximizing Samarco's financial returns,

---

[2] See our *The Age of Unproductive Capital,* https://dowbor.org/2019/06/l-dowbor-the-age-of-unproductive-capital-new-architectures-of-power-cambridge-scholars-uk-2019.html/ .

generally with short-term goals, is the only thing that matters.[3] There may be visionaries at the top of the pyramid, but these are generally people who strive to obtain the maximum possible surplus appropriation from the productive base. This is the case when, for instance, investing company assets in government bonds is considered more profitable than investing in expanding productive capacity. The logic of profitability has changed.

Capital, in its money format, was previously reinvested to expand the productive process (known as the money capital). It has now become the wealth of individuals who do not participate in the productive process. This explains a significant amount of the relative economic stagnation we see today, despite the enormous technological advances. As natural or legal persons appropriate the surplus produced in companies, what was formerly capital that fomented capital accumulation becomes potentially vast fortunes. Instead of promoting, these fortunes obstruct productive dynamics. One needs only a glance at the tables above with the top billionaires and largest companies by capitalization. The intangible economy generates an alternative form of appropriation of the surplus produced by society. This happens at a much larger scale than that of wage exploitation and, what's more, in a less conflictive manner, due to the impersonal and complex character of the system. Does anyone understand how, for instance, Henrique Meirelles generated the absurd JBS system through the J&F financial holding, moving about at ease between shady businesses in the private financing world and the Treasury Department of the world's ninth economy?[4]

Thomas Piketty's major contribution was making it perfectly clear that the system has acquired self-reproductive characteristics, due to the simple fact that financial investments yield more than investments in the real economy. The basic data show that, considering the last decades, financial investments yield an average 7% to 9% per year, while the world GDP grows on average 2 to 2.5%. The majority of the world population does not own financial investments. People spend what they earn and even more, get into debt and pay interest. Only society's economic elite has income from financial investments. These people produce little or nothing at all, but they own

[3] Samarco iron ore exploitation corporation created a huge environmental disaster in Brazil in 2015, having chosen to raise dividends to shareholders rather than investing in safer dams.

[4] The Brazilian JBS is the largest meat processing company in the world, involved in a series of financial scandals.

securities: shares, government bonds, debt and other immaterial forms of wealth. This is what we call unearned income or rent.

In other words, the dominant forms of surplus appropriation by scarcely productive or altogether unproductive minorities – the basic exploitation mechanism, to make it clear – have changed and become more sophisticated. In place of appropriation through low wages, the traditional surplus-value (which of course still exists), we now have innovative forms of appropriation generating a predominantly rentier society. This helps to understand the frail rhythm of development of the real economy, in spite of the substantial technological advances and great potential for spreading prosperity.

Appropriation of the social surplus by financial intermediaries: the unproductive capital

In *The Age of Unproductive Capital*, we delved into the profound changes in the forms of surplus appropriation.[5] We will now provide a brief account of this last study, since the form of exploitation is essential to characterize the mode of production. Taking Brazil's case as a reference, we face a deep distortion of the entire economy. This process becomes clear when we analyze the integrated financial flows: the interest rates that individuals, companies, and the public debt are charged with; the tax system with its imbalances and tax evasions; and finally, the revenue loss to tax havens. In the traditional cycle of capital accumulation, the money invested in production returned, increased by profit, and was reinvested in the productive capital. We now have a draining system that weakens the reproduction of capital, what Marjorie Kelly and Ted Howard appropriately call "extractive capitalism".

The figures are big, but not complicated. We may start from a basic reference number, our 2017 GDP, standing at 6.3 trillion *Reais*. This gives us a notion of the orders of magnitude, as simple as knowing that 630 billion *Reais* represent 10% of the GDP, and 63 billion represent 1%. Basic arithmetic makes the numbers more intelligible in our minds, given that, except for a few prosperous people, we do not handle billions on a daily basis. For example, when the big exporters and importers' tax fraud reaches the sum of 140 billion *Reais*, we are speaking of more than 2% of the GDP in tax evasion, which curiously does not make the news. Meanwhile, a

[5] L. Dowbor, *The Age of Unproductive Capital*, Cambridge Scholars Publishing, 2019 – http://dowbor.org.

meager 30 billion, assigned to the Brazilian social welfare program *Bolsa Família*, is seen as a dramatic expenditure, when it barely reaches 0.5% of the GDP. This type of yardstick for large sums is extremely useful, since economic analyses are often presented by people who love talking about large incomprehensible numbers. These billions are the result of our work as a society, and it's time to give it proper notice.

The economy has four engines: exports, household consumption, entrepreneurial investment and production, and government investment in infrastructure and the people (public policies). In Brazil, exports account for a small part: approximately 200 billion dollars, 11% of the GDP. Not much, in a country of massive dimensions, in which the internal market and activities basically represent 90% of the economic dynamics. We are not Singapore, Taiwan, or South Korea. We are a 210-million-people giant. If the internal economy fails to work, the external market may help, but it won't solve our situation. Oversimplified explanations of economic advancement and retreat based on commodity prices in the international market only camouflage the internal causes.

In the internal market, the second engine is the most important. Household consumption answers for 60% of the economy. If families don't consume, companies have no reason to produce and both will pay fewer taxes. This in turn reduces the government's capacity to invest in infrastructure and social policies. This is the vicious cycle we have been in since the coup.[6]

Household consumption dropped in 2012 and even more in 2013 and the following years due to acquired debts. The Brazilian credit protection service SPC registered 64 million adults (more than 40% of the total population) "in default" in 2018, people who were not able to pay for their previous purchases, let alone spend more. These are adults with compromised finances. If we count in their families, we are speaking of almost half the Brazilian population. The rise in debt is well documented. Family debts grew from 18.42% of total monthly income in January 2005, to 43.86% in 2013 and over 46% in 2015, with double digit interest rates.

The size of the debt would not be critical if it weren't for the applied interest rates. According to the data on interest rates presented by the National

[6] President Dilma Rousseff was ousted by a thinly disguised coup, presented as legal impeachment, formally in 2016, but the economic and political paralysis of the country started in 2014, following the attempt by Dilma to reduce interest rates that were (and still are) at usury levels.

Association of Executives of Finance, Administration and Accounting (ANEFAC), an individual paid, in February 2018, an annual rate of 129.29% on installment plans for "Household Utilities", 64.22% on personal bank loans, 297.18% on overdrafts, and 316.50% on credit card partial payments. For the sake of comparison, in France, personal bank loans cost less than 5% per year and installment plans rarely surpass the annual 10%. Brazilian interest rates are, simply put, a legalized loan shark system, made possible by the exclusion of Article 192 of the Federal Constitution. This article regulated the National Financial System through a ceiling for the real interest rate (above the inflation) of 12%, and was repelled by Congress in 2003, making usury legal.

Business loan interest rates are proportionally as scandalous as rates on personal loans. ANEFAC's study shows the average annual rate for businesses is 63.08%: 28.93% on working capital, 34.96% on factoring, and 146.83% on revolving lines of credit. No normal human being is capable of developing productive activities – starting a company, facing the time it takes to enter the market and to balance the books – with these rates. Private investments and production are directly affected.[7]

Large companies can negotiate lower tax rates with the Brazilian Development Bank (BNDES), while multinational companies enjoy annual rates below 5% in other countries. But small- to medium-sized companies are doomed to the absurd loan interest rates of the institutions where they have their business bank accounts. The entrepreneurial world, which is already paralyzed by the drop in demand, finds itself in a situation where resorting to a line of credit to withstand this critical moment is prohibitive. Moreover, with a high Selic rate, financial investments are more profitable and easier to make than investments in production. The widespread diversion of resources from production to financial investments was inevitable, aggravating still more the economic stagnation. Inflation dropped not because of some successful macroeconomic policy, but simply because, with the economic breakdown, companies began using a push strategy, and suffered losses in the process. Inflation should be balanced by financing, with cheap credit, household consumption and business investments, that is, balancing the demand with greater supply, and not by breaking both.

---

[7] Such interest rates defy credibility, but can be checked month by monthg at https://www.anefac.org/pesquisa-de-juros.

According to the Central Bank of Brazil, the household and corporate debt totaled 3.1 trillion *Reais* in 2018, almost half the GDP. Many countries have a larger debt stock, but none are charged with interest rates as high as ours. Considering individuals and companies, directed and non-directed credits, the interest flows extracted by financial intermediaries reach 1 trillion *Reais*, 16% of the GDP. This is a direct result of the absurd interest rates we saw above.

Financial intermediation is not an end but an intermediate activity. Therefore, it represents a cost. Its economic role depends on its ability to foment the economy, and with a necessarily moderate payment for it. In other words, the bank's cost/benefit relation has to be positive for the economy. On December 18, 2016, the Sunday headlines of the newspaper *O Estado de São Paulo* summarized the issue: "Credit crisis takes R$1tn from the economy and worsens the recession". During the same 12 months in which the Brazilian economy was shutting down, Itaú's profits went up 32%, and Bradesco's 25%. Americans and Europeans are shocked by our bank "spread" of 35%, a profit made without the arduous process of identifying projects, financing investments, in short, doing the homework: using the money to boost the economy instead of extorting producers and consumers.

The sufficiently critical circumstances naturally worsen with the paralysis of the fourth engine of the economy: the public investments in infrastructure and social policies. International interest rates on government bonds are between 0.5 and 1% per year. Public debt is only justified if the government's gain in financial capacity to boost the economy exceeds the costs of the debt. The Selic rate was fixed at 25% per year in July 1996, remaining at this level (it has previously reached 46%) during the Fernando Henrique Cardoso years, and around 14% in the Lula and Dilma (first mandate) years. With these rates, the public debt had become a mechanism for transferring our taxes to the bond owners. Instead of financing the government, the debt drains its resources, diverting our taxes and hindering the State's ability to foment the economy. See the data in the table below, sent to me by Nelson Barbosa:

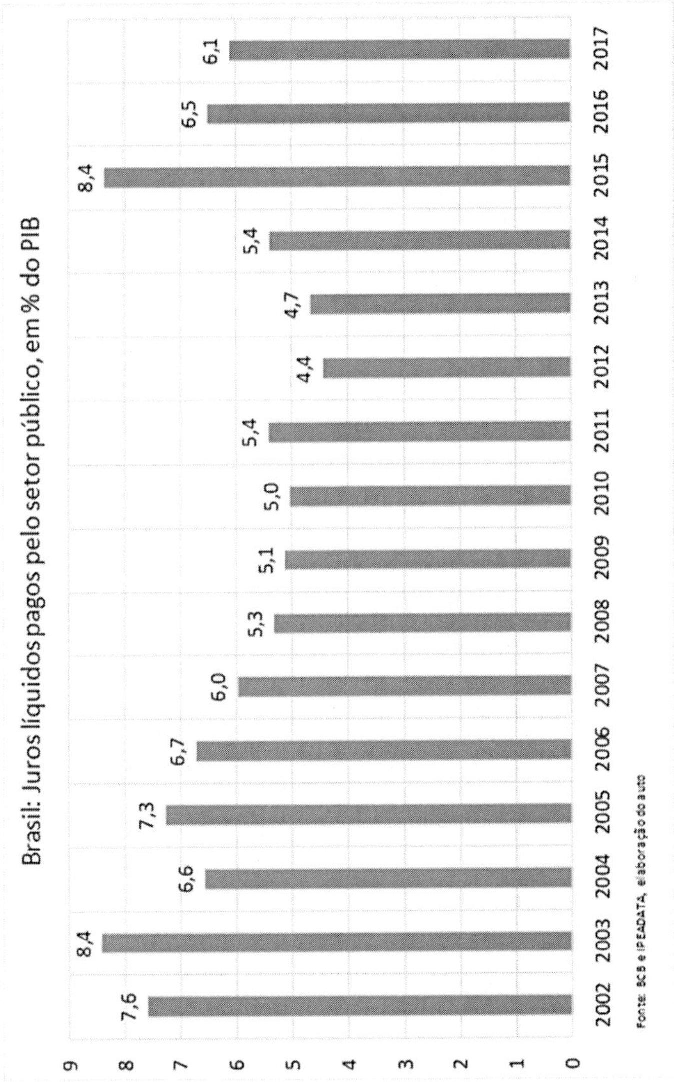

Brazil: Net interest paid by the public sector in % of the GDP

In 2015, the public debt service drained half a trillion *Reais* (8.4% of the GDP) mostly to banks, but also to international groups and of course to a portion of the upper-middle class, to whom this rate was an important part of rentism. In 2017, the amount drained was 6.1% of the GDP, a little less, but with inflation going down and the debt burden rising, the actual difference was small.

The budget deficit and the need for fiscal adjustments have been repeatedly attributed to excessive "spending" on social policies. This allegation, used to try to convince a population shocked by the recession, is a farce. The deficit was basically generated by the public debt service. The deficit in the government's activities, known as the "primary balance", never exceeded 2% of the GDP. The European Union recommends keeping the deficit below 3%. Nothing out of the ordinary. In our case, we have between 300 and 400 billion *Reais* per year that could be used in public investments to boost the economy that are largely being reapplied in the growing public debt. This is clearly the root of the budgetary crisis. The interest rate on the public debt has more recently been reduced, but the overall debt expanded, and the public debt service in 2019 cost the government 310 billion *Reais*, 10 times the Bolsa Família which took tens of millions out of extreme poverty. With impact of the pandemic, incoming 2020 figures will surely show a soaring deficit.

Public investments in infrastructure have a clear multiplying effect. But investments in social policies like health, education, security, and others are curiously seen as "expenditures". They should be considered as investments in the people. They were in fact responsible for some of the main economic miracles, particularly in Asia, but also in Finland and other countries. Families' well-being depends partly on income, the out-of-pocket economy, but also on indirect salary: Canadians may have smaller salaries than Americans, but they have universal and free access to daycare, schools, health, leisure spaces, and others. Family well-being is much higher and the economy more performative. The reduction of access to free public goods, due to resource deviation to the debt service, is a setback in terms of development. In this context, the Amendment to the Constitution 95/2016 is especially absurd, since it halts investments in public policies, but not expenditure with interests. This is by far the main source of public resource sterilization.[8]

We saw that financial intermediaries extract, in the form of interests paid by families and companies, the equivalent to 16% of the GDP. We can see that

[8] This amendment to the 1988 Constitution froze public investments in health, education and other public policies for 20 years, but not the payment of interest on the public debt. In an unequal country such as Brazil, this has dramatic consequences, particularly with the 2020 pandemic.

part of our taxes, ranging around 6% to 8% of the GDP, depending on the year, is also transformed in interest through the public debt. This means that, in real terms, the debt-drain continues. If we join the three, the drains that deplete family demands, company investment capacity, and the State's investment capacity, we are talking of over 20% of sterilized GDP. No economy can thrive like this.

There are other places where resources are underused. Pension funds, for instance, manage an accumulated resource stock in the order of a trillion *Reais* (16% of the GDP). In many countries, the sector is regulated so that resources are reinvested productively, raising production so it may cover the future needs of retired people. In Brazil, these funds may be 100% applied in government bonds. The complementary pension of the wealthier portion of society is in this way substantially financed by everyone's taxes, and particularly from the poorest, who pay proportionally more taxes.

There are similar distortions in other sectors, particularly insurance. But we are interested in the integrated flow, the radical distortion of the country's system of financial intermediation, which instead of financing the economy and boosting productive investments, generates intermediation costs for everyone. Gerald Epstein and Juan Antônio Montecino, from the Roosevelt Institute, in a research study on the United States' integrated financial flows, showed the "negative net productivity of high finance".[9] Instead of serving the economy, financial intermediaries make use of it. Americans popularly say that today *the tail is wagging the dog.*

Most functioning countries, when faced with this distortion, strive to recover balance through the tax system. Our system not only fails to correct but aggravates the imbalance. In Brazil, 50% of the tax burden is charged on consumption in the form of indirect taxes. Given that the poorest transform income almost entirely into consumption, they pay proportionally more taxes. The case of the tax law exempting profit and dividends is particularly ominous. The law passed on December 26, 1995, clearly favors the wealthiest segment of the social pyramid. This, together with the absence of wealth taxation, the minimal costs of inheritance taxes, the low taxation on higher amounts of income, and the virtual inexistence of the

---

[9] Gerald Epstein and Juan Antonio Montecino – Overcharged: the high cost of high finance – The Roosevelt Institute, July 2016
– http://rooseveltinstitute.org/overcharged-high-cost-high-finance/

Rural Land Tax (ITR), shows our tax system deeply aggravates the distortion. It amounts to an organized system for rewarding the unproductive.

The economic power of the wealthiest, especially of banks, has become political power, opening the way for a still greater resource drain. The National Union of Public Attorneys of the National Treasury (Sinprofaz) estimates a tax evasion of around 600 billion *Reais*. The evasion is evidently not from wage-earners, whose tax is deducted from the payroll and who pay taxes included in the products they buy. It comes from the richest. They not only fail to invest but drain the economy without even paying the due taxes. All large banks and financial institutions have technical departments to aid in tax evasion through procedures called "fiscal optimization". They also have branches in tax havens. Paulo Guedes, the present minister of the economy, is co-founder of BTG Pactual bank, which has 38 affiliates in tax havens.[10]

What was left of Article 192 of the Constitution stipulates that "The national financial system, [shall be] structured to promote the balanced development of the country and to serve the collective interests". We are used to calling diversion, theft, or corruption things that are considered illegal. But the reality is that the great corruption, the truly substantial money diversion in terms of economic imbalance, today has enough political strength to generate its own legality. This is done through minor laws that simply ignore the duty to "promote the balanced development of the country". Those who manage our financial flows have ceased to "serve the collective interests" and become a barrier in their way. Interest rates that would be deemed usury in any country or circumstance and consequently forbidden are perfectly legal here. What do you call the act of taking over resources produced by a third party without a corresponding productive contribution?

The extraction of society's surplus production by financial intermediaries and other rentists has impressive dimensions. These proportions are possible largely because the mechanisms of financial regulation are situated at the national level, while finances are global-scaled. Currency is now a magnetic signal, traveling the world with immense volatility. It is no longer printed by governments; it is immaterial and emitted by banks. Society has a very limited ability to control its flows; and much less so of directing them to productive activities. The Global Financial Integrity, on its study about

[10] For the list of these tax havens, see https://dowbor.org/2019/04/l-dowbor-de-onde-vem-o-nosso-super-ministro-da-economia-6p.html/; See also The Economist, December 15, 2018, p. 65.

Brazil, estimates that the leakages to foreign grounds through under-invoicing and over-invoicing (in this case, genuinely illegal, fraudulent practices), cost the country approximately 35 billion dollars a year, almost 2% of the GDP. The Tax Justice Network estimates that the Brazilian resource stock in tax havens reached the mark of 520 billion dollars in 2012, equal to 26% of the GDP at the time. Of this amount, less than 3% have been repatriated, in a much-publicized effort to bring the money home.

Brazil's financial economy leaks from all sides. We are not the only ones facing the hardships of unproductive financialization. As we saw, in the last decades, financial investments have yielded around 7% to 9% a year, while the GDP grows between 2 and 2.5%. Financial flows go, of course, to where they yield more, and it is not in production, since financial investments yield more than productive ones. In Brazil, the system is just much more distorted. Financialization leads to more rentism and aggravates the absurd wealth concentration.

Our problem has never been of fiscal adjustment. If we add up the stagnation in household consumption and entrepreneurial productive activity, the deviation of public resources to the debt service, the aggravations created by the tax burden structure, tax evasion, leakage to foreign countries and the widespread use of tax havens, we have, without a doubt, a dysfunctional economy. We are not hoping for a miracle here. Our goal is to show that at the center of a functional economy is the ground zero of economics: the rational allocation of resources. The actual rule of thumb is that the remuneration of economic agents should be to some extent proportional to their contribution to the economy. We must reward the ones that multiply wealth the most, not those who drain it better. By presenting the integrated financial flow, we aim to show that solutions are systemic and require a new agreement for development. The time when "liquidity" was the currency issued by the government is gone. In the era of immaterial currency, most emissions come from financial institutions in the form of credit, more than 90%, private creation of money.

In general terms, Brazil's case shows that the financial system has become a mechanism for surplus extraction even more powerful than wage exploitation, inverting the global tendency of inequality reduction that lasted thirty years of the post-war period. This generates, in fact, accumulated impacts, since wages and social rights are being affected by the demands of financial profit. The form of surplus extraction and the exploitation of the peoples, which are central characteristics of a mode of production, are changing. In terms of social productivity, the debt lords are not very different from the feudal lords: they live off the efforts of others. But the magnitude of exploitation is of a much higher order, and the mechanism of social surplus appropriation has changed.

The growing inequality

The change is systemic not only because exploitation has intensified (it now accumulates both salary and financial exploitation), but also because financial rent is a burden on the productive system. The traditional producer from the shoe factory, for example, would exploit workers, but the result to society would be more (albeit ill-paid) employment; machinery and raw material demands; shoes for the population; and taxes for government to finance infrastructure and social policies. The guiding axis was profit.

In financial capitalism, as we saw, the guiding axis is the dividend, the profitability of securities. It is important to distinguish productive investments from financial investments. Banks, for obvious reasons, call everything investments; it seems nobler. But the 1% who control most of the world's resources do not invest, in the sense of generating new productive capacity. The rate of return on securities may be high, but it does not result in a new pair of shoes or a new house. The guiding axis of financial capitalism is the dividend and other forms of rent. This generates a new logic for the capitalist edifice.

The remarkable ability that a minority has of appropriating the surplus of society's production constitutes a cumulative process. I like to use an image provided to me by Susan George. A capitalist who invests a billion dollars to earn a meager 5% a year is earning 137 thousand dollars a day. As it is impossible to spend this amount of money, they will reinvest most of it, generating a cumulative process called the snowball effect. The poor spend, the rich "invest". The middle class tries to tag along by making small investments and hoping for rentism to prosper.[11]

The terrifying new inequality cycle has been made clear by Thomas Piketty's studies. But what helped size this cycle was a supplementary study on wealth concentration, rather than income. This study, which analyzed wealth concentration, was initially conducted by the UN, then further developed by the Credit Suisse, and later disclosed to the entire world by Oxfam. In Brazil, six people have more wealth than the poorer half of the population, and 5% have a larger share than the other 95%. As for the whole

[11] Concerning the snowball effect, see Julian Sims, *How money works* (p. 208).

world, 8 families have more wealth than the poorer half of the population (3.7 billion), and 1% have more patrimony than the remaining 99%.

The 2018 Oxfam report for the World Economic Forum in Davos confirms we are rapidly going backwards:

> Inequality is rising. Eighty-two percent of the wealth generated last year went to the richest one percent of the global population, while the 3.7 billion people who make up the poorest half of the world saw no increase in their wealth. Our broken economy is increasing the gap between the rich and the poor. This allows a small elite to accumulate vast wealth at the cost of hundreds of millions of people, frequently women, who fight for survival with poor incomes and basic rights denied. (Oxfam, 2018)

Inequality seemed a well-trodden subject. But it is not just a question of injustice: it is a mechanism that halts the economy, generates social convulsion, and disorganizes society as a whole. We are far beyond the realm of productive companies' traditional surplus-value. To exploit workers by means of low salaries, you at least have to give them jobs, and generate production. Financial surplus-value allows exploiting governments through public debt and companies and individuals as well. This produces a class of financial intermediaries who not only fail to finance production, consumption, and public investments – the engines of the economy – but paralyze them. We are in the era of the unproductive accumulation of wealth, of the decapitalization of society. This is a systemic dismantling. The reform of the global (and, in Brazil, national) financial system is the central challenge. Wealth concentration without a productive counterpart, "unearned income", in the English terminology, produces rich rentists and halted economies. Not to mention, of course, the increasing political chaos.

Above a certain level, inequality produces dysfunctional economies and societies. In ethical terms, the numbers are simply scandalous: nearly a billion people suffer from hunger, out of which more than 150 million are children. Lack of access to basic medication, clean water, basic infrastructure, and electricity, in the 21st century, is utterly shameful. Channeling resources to relieve people in despair should be an evident priority to any decent human being. Given the current situation, labeling any sign of indignation as "populism" or "leftism" is absurd. Hunger is not orthodox or heterodox, its existence is shameful, particularly to the richest.

Inequality is also absurd in economic terms. Firstly, because tackling the multiple effects of inequality and misery is much more costly than systematically providing access to the basic needs for a dignified life for all.

Inequality is especially absurd when we consider that, by depriving the majority of the population of consumption, income and wealth concentration halt productive processes because of lowered demand levels. As we've seen in the Brazilian case, the economic strangling at the basis of society, produced by the financial system, led to the collapse of the productive system. Since the State depends on consumption and production for revenue, investments in infrastructure and public policies halted. Functioning economies are based on a reasonably balanced distribution of society's resources, and this is valid for nearly all cases of economic success in the world.

Inequality also deters political processes, creating societies in permanent conflict. Wealth concentration allows dominant groups to take over the government, the judicial branch, and the media, depriving the State of its central function of reconstituting political, social, and economic balance. Privatizations disorganize the general functioning of society. In the national spheres, frightening discourses emerge. People like Trump are elected, decisions like Brexit are voted. Not to mention the case of Brazil, with the coup and the election of a political aberration. In the international sphere, Europe is surrounding itself with barbed wire fences, Trump battled to build a gigantic wall at the Mexican frontier, and Israel confines Palestinians in controlled zones which increasingly resemble concentration camps. It would be smarter to make use of the huge demand potential in these populations to boost the economy as a whole.

Today it is clear there will be no peace or balance on our small planet until we reach a Global New Deal for inclusive development. The report of the United Nations Conference on Trade and Development (UNCTAD) is explicit:

> No social or economic order is safe if it fails to ensure a fair distribution of its benefits in good times and the costs in bad times. Insisting that 'there is no alternative' is yesterday's political slogan. People everywhere desire much the same thing: a decent job, a secure home, a safe environment, a better future for their children and a government that listens and responds to their concerns; in truth, they want a different deal from that offered by hyperglobalization. The 2030 Agenda for Sustainable Development, Trade and Development Report 2017 II codified in a series of goals, targets and indicators, points in that direction.

It is my conviction that until a larger number of people understand the mechanisms that distort our development, there will not be enough strength for the transformations. We have the advantage that what works in the economy is simple: a systematic fight against inequality and environmental imbalance. This time around, whatever the pact, it will have to "lift all boats", both developing and developed countries, and stand up to the global challenges that hinder a sustainable and inclusive development. "*Prosperity for all cannot be delivered by austerity-minded politicians, rent-seeking corporations and speculative bankers. What is urgently needed now is a global new deal*" (Unctad, 2017, ii, emphasis added, LD).

The exploitation system has, therefore, become broader and more sophisticated. The gains in productivity that result from the broad scientific and technological revolution could guarantee a steady growth in production and widespread prosperity. But the majority of the population is cut off from the gains to which they are entitled. They accumulate three forms of exploitation: low wages, abusive interest rates, and restricted access to public goods of collective consumption, such as health, education, security, and others. And financial corporate giants exploit productive companies through dividend extraction. In this context, the dominant system not only increasingly dismisses democracy, but tends to evolve to more violent forms of social control and coercion to remain in power. The transformations in the world of work help to understand the erosion of society's capacity to resist.

The shift in work relations

In former times, and this is still the case for rural producers, the house was on the cultivated land. Living and working happened in the same place and the whole family took part. Boys and girls of a young age would help. The industrial era led to a rural exodus, and cities grew around the great productive units, the power plants, factories, and offices. Workers began to rent out their workforce for certain hours a day, during which they would do as they were told. Individually, people began developing productive abilities and offering their services for rent by the hour, day, or month, depending on the circumstances. This is known as employment.

Employment bonds, which still seem to us the natural form of making a living and sustaining our families, are changing, and not for ideological reasons. The technology-dense society of knowledge is changing work relations. Robert Reich, in *The Future of Success*, suggests that the traditional wage work will have lasted a total of 150 years, and will be substituted by other types of relations. Without going as far as Jeremy Rifkin's *The End of Work*, the fact is, work relations are shifting according to some big lines that are becoming clear.

Just as in the Industrial Revolution, the ongoing technological revolution generates a gap between the sophisticated and creative work of those who organize and manage the system and the work of those who follow instructions. The latter are increasingly being substituted by automation, robotics, and artificial intelligence. In *The Future of Professions: how technology will transform the work of human experts*, Richard and Daniel Susskind claim this tendency will include architects, lawyers, economists, and other similar professionals. The intellectual work of first-rate lawyers will continue developing, but the high demand for young jurists, for researching court rulings and organizing information in the large law firms, will tend to disappear. Everything is online now and can be found through algorithm-based intelligent search mechanisms.

> For example, to some extent at least, tax advisers are already being disintermediated by online tax preparation software, lawyers by document assembly systems, doctors by diagnostic apps, teachers by MOOCs, architects by online CAD systems, and journalists by bloggers. (121)

The process aggravates another preexistent dynamic: informal work. We check on the unemployment statistics so much that we forget what they mean. If we take Brazil, for example, unemployment rates are currently estimated at 14% of the economically active population. But there is an equally bad or even worse hidden form of unemployment, represented by the people who do not declare themselves as part of the workforce because they gave up trying, leaving the economically active population for hopelessness. There is also the growing number of people who survive on the "organized odd job". These are the dreadful transition activities, such as in call centers. This is also the vast world of outsourced precarious jobs. Generally speaking, we must consider the huge population in the informal sector – about 40 million in Brazil – who "make ends meet" in the most varied manners. Informal labor reaches 30% to 40% in Latin America and 70% in North African countries. These are people who never become fully employed, whose hopes of insertion in the formal labor market diminish as technologies develop. This new era is characterized by significant underuse of the world population's productive capacity, under the poorly-argued allegation that it's not the system that is failed, but the people that lack adequate "employability", who are claimed to be "unemployable".

Even in the more sophisticated environments of creative work, having an employee at the work table for eight hours a day might not be the best option for the company. A large portion of office work is already being done at home. Tracking work hours and having the worker physically present are not as important now as the network of connected workers, wherever they may be located. The pandemic is clearly accelerating this trend. The German White Paper on the impact of the digital era on work suggests that it is "widely expected that the platform economy will lead to an increase in self-employment, especially solo self-employed persons, who can offer their services and products simply and inexpensively via platforms" (Friedrich Ebert Stiftung, 9). André Gorz uses the concept of the "self-entrepreneur":

> Big firms will now retain only a small core of stable full-time employees. The rest of 'their' personnel – 90 percent in the case of the hundred largest American companies – will be formed from a variable mass of external collaborators, agency and temporary workers, genuinely or falsely self-employed persons, as well as high-flying professionals. The company can dump an increasing part of the costs (of the value) of their workforce. (Gorz, 24)

In attempting to address the future of work, we are still moving cautiously. But what we realize, in broad terms, is a deep shift in the fundamental axis of traditional capitalism formed by the work relations. Unions and workers have significantly lost strength to face the exploitation mechanisms. In the fragmented and hierarchical world of work, creating solidarity movements has become harder. Brazil is an ironic case; the coup has been a setback, in terms of guarantees and safeties, when what we need precisely is to protect and expand our rights and recover the pace of development. In my view, the solutions are in the new forms of insertion that the knowledge economy has opened.

The cognitive capital logic

We saw that in the knowledge economy, the use of the main factor of production doesn't reduce its stock. In other terms, it is possible to socialize it universally without generating additional costs. This causes a deep change in the logic of capitalism. On the relation between the cognitive capital and the logic of value, Gorz writes:

> The term 'knowledge economy' means significant trouble to the economic system. It indicates that knowledge has become the main productive force; that, as a consequence, the products of social activity are no longer chiefly crystallized labor but crystallized knowledge; and that the exchange value of commodities, material or otherwise, is no longer determined in the last instance by the quantity of general social labor they contain but mainly by their content in terms of general information, knowledge and intelligence. It is the last element, and not abstract social labor, measurable according to

> a single standard, that has become the main social substance common to all commodities. It has become the main source of value and profit, and in this way, according to varied authors, the main form of labor and capital. (29)

With this, we are deeply altering the theory of value, which was based on the relatively homogeneous cost of the workforce and surplus-value.

> The heterogeneity of so-called 'cognitive' labor activities, of the immaterial products that they create and the capacities and knowledge they imply, makes both the value of the labor force or its product immeasurable. (…) The crisis of the measurement of labor-time inevitably engenders a crisis in the measurement of value. (29)

Gar Alperovitz and Lew Daly present a similar view, in their excellent *Unjust Deserts*:

> Dividing the economic cake – even if through a rough approximation of contributions and rewards, as many other bargain situations try to do – becomes extremely difficult when we understand, regarding growth, the centrality of the contributions based on historic knowledge. Who or what generates growth – in any morally relevant sense is, to say the least, a more complicated issue. All of this, suggested Daniel Bell, requires a new 'knowledge theory of value', especially as we move deeper into the high-tech sphere. (Alperovitz, 64)[12]

As knowledge develops, it can be indefinitely assimilated into more activities, with no additional costs. This characteristic is the basis of the 'zero marginal cost economy', according to Rifkin. As this tendency grows, the war of capital to create value moves to a new place. It strives to make the main factor of production, knowledge, scarce. This is the main reason behind the increasing number of rights over intellectual property, such as copyrights, patents, royalties, and other fees. This is how the private appropriation of the means of production is done when the means are immaterial and can, by nature, be freely accessed. When a factor of production is abundant, there is no way for a company to extract exchange value from it, just as there is no way for charging access to air. Instead of generalizing free access to new knowledge and thus guaranteeing a much broader social value, the capital strives to restrict access, since scarcity generates a higher exchange value. Enzo Rullani, in *Le capitalisme cognitif,* shows this clearly: "The value of knowledge is then entirely linked to the practical ability to restrict its free diffusion, to create legal constraints –

[12] Alperovitz and Daly refer to the Daniel Bell classic – *The coming of the Post-Industrial Society,* Basic Books, New York 1990 [1973].

patents, copyrights, licenses, contracts – or monopolize the ability to copy, to imitate, to reinvent, to learn skills of others" (in Gorz, 36).

The vast amounts of resources accumulated by the pharmaceutical giants, for instance, originate mainly from restricting the right to produce essential medication for society, when the costs of production and the corresponding profit have already been widely covered (Angell). From this level on, as Stiglitz defends, it is a question of rentism, of "unearned income". The additional costs to society will in turn be transformed into financial income, as we saw above. It is fundamental to note here that this cognitive capitalism contributes less to generating access than to generating artificial scarcity. Oligopoly in the place of market competition, scarcity in the place of abundance, and rentism in the place of production profit.

The roles of economic subjects change. What links us to the system today is less the exchange between producers and consumers, on opposite ends of a transaction that involves actual goods and services, than the virtual flow of intangible assets. We are now connected through platforms, and using the platforms like everyone else is mandatory, otherwise, we become isolated. I have to use WhatsApp because everyone else does, or Microsoft Word, or others. This is what we call a monopoly created from demand. We have to use what others use. This opens the way for the platform controllers to charge disproportionate values relative to the contribution they give. The private appropriation of people's communications in global platforms, the data collected on our tastes, relationships, thoughts, illnesses, and so many other personal details, generates a new relationship between the actors in the economic process.

Douglas Heaven summarizes:

> Facebook, Google, Apple and Amazon variously avoid tax, crush competition and violate privacy, the complaints go. Their inscrutable algorithms determine what we see and what we know, shape opinions, narrow world views and even subvert the democratic order that spawned them. In 2018, a 'techlash' is in full flow. There is broad agreement that something must be done about big tech (…) Whether it is Amazon's 'customers who bought this also bought' function, or the eye-catching red or orange 'something new' dots on your smartphone app icons, big tech's products are not just good, but subtly designed to control us, even to addict us — to grab us by the eyeballs and hold us there. The result is the attention economy, whose coin is data.

Knowledge is becoming the main factor of production; the effective determination of value is increasingly fluid; new mechanisms are appearing for controlling intellectual property; access platforms are growing to gigantic proportions; and the social surplus appropriation is now through virtual money, magnetic signals with unlimited accumulation. We are changing the structure of what we call capitalism. This capitalism not only concentrates wealth, as we saw earlier, but particularly blocks the potentials for the expansion of social wealth. To society, the losses, or what we cease to earn due to barred access to knowledge and its potential multiplying effects, are incomparably greater than the profit squeezed-out by those who block access.

On a change-driven note, "this means that for the first time the main productive force, and main source of value, can lie beyond private appropriation" (Gorz, 37). The nature of the war over the social surplus, over the wealth we produce, has changed. The privatization of universities, student debts, oligopolies of scientific journals, and persecutions on open access are part of a battle to create a hierarchy in access to education. This is part of a new world of fights. Access to knowledge is liberating. To the oligarchies, the issue is controlling knowledge. To us, it is a question of transforming education, technology, and culture, in a global process of interactive and collaborative construction. The attempt to regulate knowledge through private appropriation and market mechanisms simply does not work. It is different from car sales. This type of logic blocks creativity instead of making good use of its multiplying effects.

The shift in market mechanisms

The market is an essential but far from sufficient regulatory mechanism. As a free competition mechanism, it makes sense to determine prices and quantities based on supply and demand. In terms of structuring productive processes, the same functioning assumes that the profit of the producer is the result of an adequate answer to society's needs, which appear as demand. This type of market can be seen in a variety of consumer goods produced by different competitors, from shoes to automobiles to pizzas. But the reality today is that these goods and services, where competition actually plays a part, are a thinning slice of economic activities.

In the broader spectrum, we have corporate gigantism. When we look at the previously mentioned 147 groups that control 40% of the world corporate system, or the 16 giant traders that control most commodities in the world, or even the 28 SIFIs (*Systemically Important Financial Institutions*), it is impossible not to realize this is a power structure. We studied this structure in *The Age of Unproductive Capital*. Here, we are interested in the fact that giants of this size today are formed of interconnected systems. They generate an enormous space where prices are managed. The named competition "to better serve the client" remains only in a few segments of the economy, in the scope of small- and medium-sized companies. The new context naturally did not exclude the war between the groups, a war that fuels the giants in the legal industry, a fierce fight to appoint government officials and central bank presidents, to control media segments or even the judiciary.

The market in its original sense survives in the crevices, and any significant competitor that tries to enter the upper hall is simply destroyed, like Netscape, or bought, like Instagram and WhatsApp, or even subcontracted by the larger group. We are facing a monumental power pyramid, in which the executives, as we call them, have essentially become political operators. Those who point an angry finger at corrupt politicians forget that today they are largely only representatives of the corruptors. This is the "Cover-State", which permits the policies imposed by corporations to appear as unpopular initiatives of the government; a useful but innocuous lightning rod for the population's rage. As Luc Anderssen vehemently states, politicians exist so we may think we have a choice.[13]

Another highly significant change in large corporations is the tension between the company technicians and managers on one side and the major shareholders on the other. While the first may be interested in the long-term balance and economic and social utility of what they do, the latter, who we call the institutional investors, the financial sphere as a whole, have short-term interests. Lynn Stout wrote a telling book on this conflict, *The Shareholder Value Myth*. She wrote especially about the myth that corporations are legally bound to defend the interests of the shareholders. The author demonstrates this is much more a cultural and political construction than properly a legal obligation. This culture is an ally to institutional investors' gigantism. It produces a situation in which the interests of the major investors, who invest in financial securities, overpower the companies' long-term views, which would be in favor of the company itself, the employees, the communities, and the environment. The dismantling of *Petrobras* in favor of the dominant interests of international financial investors is just one more example.

---

13 See Luc Anderssen's three impressive minutes on our real spaces of choice. https://m.facebook.com/pg/prof.LadislauDowbor/videos/?ref=page_internal&mt_nav=0.

No financial operator will understand the actual impact of "a conglomerate that sells everything, from pet food to airplane engines and financial services" (69). They will only consider the investments' profitability rates. British Petroleum well defended the interests of greater profitability of its shareholders, but generated immense external costs to the sea life of the Gulf of Mexico, to the local fishing industry, to tourism and to coastal cities.

> Under pressure from the American government in the wake of the *Deepwater Horizon* oil spill, BP announced it would suspend paying its regular dividends. This sparked a firestorm of protests from British pensioners who relied on BP dividends for retirement income. BP agreed to quickly resume paying dividends after announcing plans to sell off approximately $30 billion in assets, including many BP oil fields. (Stout, 84)

That is, maintaining the dividends, even if by decapitalizing the company.

The frantic search to maximize profit and satisfy the institutional investors has led to technological underinvestment, multiplied risks, and losses to all the actors involved, including the company's base capital. The systemic and long-term interests have been left aside. The list of examples here is interminable: medication fraud (GSK), fraud involving implants (Johnson & Johnson), food being jam-packed with pesticides and antibiotics (Bayer and numerous other companies), fraud on interest rates (all large banks, without exception), technical and legal support for tax evasion and money laundering (virtually all large financial intermediaries), data fraud on pollutant emissions (VW and many others), sales of contaminated children's milk (Lactalis) and so many others. The reader may pick any large company, "GSK" for instance, and add "settlements" to an internet query to find their criminal record. As the *Economist* commented, to large companies, "it has become increasingly difficult to abide by the law".

The gap between the interests of consumers, society, and the environment on one side and the short-term financial interests on the other is becoming wider. What we call the market is not the market anymore, but rather a political, financial, and legal (if not military) structure that disorganizes the economy. In economic terms, Lynn Stout uses a strong image: "When the interests of investors in short and long term diverge, the shareholder mentality in terms of value places the same risks as dynamite fishing. Some individuals may gain immense and immediate results. But, as a whole and with time, the investors and the economy lose" (73). And this, despite the researchers and those who organize productive processes assuring us of the immense technological advances. We don't lack the technical or financial means, but the political guidance to use them.

***

We've seen up until now the transformations in the productive base of society, with the evolution into a society of knowledge that is intangible to some, immaterial to others, but essentially anchored in magnetic signals. In the era of global connectivity, with the internet, smartphones, and other mechanisms for stocking, managing, and transmitting knowledge, the very logic of capitalism has changed. Having changed, the technical basis generates, in turn, a set of social relations of production that affect both the labor world – with new hierarchies, work relations, and forms of exploitation – and the corporate world, with the gigantic platforms which we are all condemned to navigate. The very dematerialization of money and its volatility in the virtual space has particularly shifted and deeply amplified the forms of surplus extraction. The organizational basis of capitalism has deeply changed. But with it, the forms of power and dominant ideologies, what we call the system's superstructures, equally change.

III –

THE SYSTEM'S SUPERSTRUCTURES

The truth is that Margaret Thatcher's definitive world of 1980, along the lines of *There is no alternative*, with national democracies, elections, local markets, and foreign trade, is rapidly leaving the stage. The infrastructures, the productive basis of the world, are changing, and because of this the superstructures, the set of rules inherited from the era of the economy of the nations, become deeply misadjusted. The planet has shrunk, we must all search for sustainable development goals, the nations must settle for a reduced role, the peoples must learn to live in a multicultural environment. And, far beyond a Welfare State, we must evolve, as UNCTAD says, towards a *Global New Deal*, a new global pact, because the current disruption is leading the world to deep environmental, social, political and economic dramas.

As a whole, society's formal mechanisms for regulation and domination, at the superstructural level, are still to a large extent rooted in the era of industrial and competitive capitalism. The corporate activities are rapidly outlining a new organizational architecture. The new forms of organizing power in society generate spaces of global governance that escape the formal national systems. Corporate political power is opening spaces for a massive erosion of the public dimensions of the State. Knowledge is appropriated as if the final product were an individual creation or a personal physical good. A powerful ideological discourse strives to generalize the narrative of the merit and legitimacy of the new forms of power. A capillary vigilance over the population at the level of individual privacy can lead to a radical loss of freedom. This is especially true for those who by chance do not believe in the "narrative".

World governance

The capitalism we inherited from the last century was still the capitalism of the nations. Of course, we have had global capitalism since the commercial revolution of the 16th century, or since the 19th and 20th centuries' imperialist stage. We have studies on progressive globalization throughout history, by

Rudolf Hilferding, Lenin, and, in the post-war period, by Samir Amin, with his insightful masterpiece, *Accumulation on a world scale*. Besides these, numerous studies have focused on finance, commodities, culture, or other specific dimensions. But we can now say that the capitalism of the nations is disappearing from the face of the Earth, given that decision-making has shifted to the hands of this monstrous network full of tentacles that the corporate giants form. They are inside national governments as well, and with very little interest in the nations where they are lodged.

In the absence of a global government, in the political sense of a legitimate and representative government, the only system to hold power in an organized manner at the global level is formed by the corporations, the financial giants much more than the productive corporations. None of this is entirely new, but we can say that from the 1980s on, and more rapidly after the 2008 crisis, we have undergone a qualitative change. This is not a country's corporations controlling that country's politics. These are global groups controlling, in an organized manner, a set of countries simultaneously, with the ability to change national laws according to their transnational interests.

All large corporations have solid connections with tax havens and can move their resources without the least control of the public sphere and the elected governments. With uncontrolled international flows, the possibility governments had of charging taxes and channeling resources productively is reduced. A characteristic example is the meager 0.05% that Apple paid on taxes over their monumental profits in Europe, in 2016. José Antonio Ocampo provides a clear synthesis:

> Globalization has made the international regime of business taxation obsolete. The current scheme was created by the developed countries of the early 20th century. Back then, their companies dominated world trade – essentially focused on goods – and formed integrated societies, doing business with companies established in other countries or colonies. But today, almost half the world trade happens between the head offices and branches of transnational companies, the service sector represents three fifths of the world GDP, and the developing countries produce two fifths of the product. Their large companies are also transnational. (36)

Economic news headlines show the fight between the European Union and the United States concerning taxes on companies. What really matters, though, is that the loss in tax returns reduces governments' capacity to promote development through investments in infrastructures and social policies. If we do not govern the resources for financing policies, do we govern politics? A capitalism in which the economy is global and regulations are national simply blocks governments' ability to perform their main function of balancing development through economic policies. In the context of global financial flows, Keynesian national policies largely cease to work. The long-term predicted by Keynes has arrived.

From 2012 to 2013, the Dilma administration tried to reduce the utterly criminal interest rates that were strangling the economy to the benefit of financial rentism. Her government didn't last. From mid-2013 onwards, we have been ravaged by a political, mediatic, and legal war. The upper middle class, with its investments and easy rentism, relentlessly reacted. The government that resulted from the coup put two private banks in charge of public resources. The economic and political mess smoothed the path for opportunists from the far-right. This situation is not unique to us. The American government paid trillions of dollars to their big banks, and the European Union paid trillions of Euros to theirs. Both kept their rentists satisfied with what is called *Quantitative Easing*. Those who tried to escape the financial trap, like Greece, were the target of a concentrated attack. In February 2018, Trump generously presented the corporate world with reductions in taxes from 35% to 20%, while the United States plunged in inequality. These are mere illustrations from recent times of the profound transformation we are undergoing.

Appropriation of the public sphere by the corporate system

No news here. In the capitalist system, the State serves the interests of the capitalists. But when the Exxon CEO becomes the US Secretary of State (he had to sever all ties with the company to comply with the conflict-of-interest requirements, which earned him a 125-million-dollar compensation. He didn't last long, as was typical in the Trump era), or Goldman Sachs executives become the American government's top economic advisors, not to mention the former resident's profile as a real estate speculator himself, we are seeing qualitative changes. In Brazil, besides being responsible for the 2013 crisis, the large financial groups run the Ministry of Treasury and the Central Bank. With the 2018 elected government, a super ministry of economy is run by bankers. The big picture outlined and taught in the universities – the division of powers and the checks and balances – has been surpassed. Companies are in power, and financial giants control the companies. Corporate power is not an entrepreneurial power in parallel with political power. It is political power itself. The CEOs of the large groups are engaged in politics day and night.

We examined in detail the process through which corporations hijack political power in the previously mentioned *The era of unproductive capital*. We will here resume some of its key points to provide a broad view of what we suggest to be a new mode of production, without the reader having to refer to the previous text. The basic element is that we have organized global finance facing the fragmented political power of 200 nations; besides this, the power within nations, in its different dimensions, is being fractured by dissent and is easily captured. We are becoming systemically dysfunctional.

Wolfgang Streeck provides an insightful systematization of the capture of public power by corporations at the governmental level. With government debt as a means of control together with the other mechanisms that we saw earlier, a process is generated in which the government must increasingly answer to the market and turn its back on citizenship. A government's survival now chiefly depends on its ability to satisfy the markets and the financial interests sufficiently to be deemed "trustworthy". The interests of the population that elected that government become secondary. Instead of a republic, a *res publica*, or public affair, we have a *res mercatori*, a market affair. A summary table can help us understand the radical shift in politics (p. 81):[14]

Citizen's State	**Market's State**
national	international
citizens	investors
civil rights	contractual rights
voters	creditors
elections (periodic)	auctions (continuous)
public opinion	interest rates
loyalty	"trustworthiness"
public services	debt service

Naturally, one is financed through taxes and the other through credit. A government thus becomes dependent on "two environments that place contradictory demands on its behavior" (p. 80). Public opinion will judge the quality of the government, while something we mysteriously qualify as "the markets" will place a "risk evaluation" based, for instance, on the government's ability to pay high interest rates on debt, or use Quantitative

[14] Wolfgang Streeck, *Buying time,* Verso, London, 2014 http://dowbor.org/category/dicas-de-leitura/.

Easing. Between one and the other, political survival lies increasingly with the latter. In the place of the welfare state and the public policies, now we have austerity and financial profit. The important thing is having "the market's trust", being "market friendly".

To Streeck, this is not the end of capitalism, but of democratic capitalism. We may naturally solve our taxonomy problem by adding qualifiers to our studied animal, such as global capitalism or authoritarian capitalism. We can likewise qualify it according to its stages, referring to the third or fourth industrial revolution, or to financial capitalism. Furthermore, we can think of the changes represented by the expansion of informational factors of production. Another fundamental aspect is the change in the forms of social surplus appropriation, in the case of financial rentism exceeding production profits. But the essential aspect we are searching for is the systemic logic that results from the various changes. The question that must be asked is whether the category *capitalism* still applies to the whole set. Capitalism has always been exploitative, but it had the positive connotation of a vector for productive accumulation. Today, these dimensions are dissociated.

Knowledge appropriation

The private appropriation of a social product must be justified. The main contribution of Alperovitz and Daly, in the small book *Unjust Deserts*, is making clear how certain minorities take over the collective efforts of knowledge construction. In making these mechanisms clear to us, the authors are developing a theory of value of the knowledge economy with strong explanatory power concerning the modern society. Their analysis is a type of antidote against the new fairy tale that says the economy will do well if "the markets" – meaning the big financial groups – are satisfied.

In an example given by the authors, when Monsanto gains exclusivity over a given seed, as if the technological innovation was only their contribution, they forget the process behind these advances.

> What they do not have to consider ever is the huge collective investment that brought genetic science from its isolated beginnings to the point at which the company makes its decision. All the biological, statistical, and other knowledge without which none of today's highly productive and disease-resistant seeds could be developed – and all of the publication, research, education, training, and related technical devices without which learning and knowledge could not have been communicated and nurtured at each particular stage of development, and then passed on over time and

> embodied, too, in a trained labor force of technicians and scientists – all of this comes to the company free of charge, a gift of the past. (55)

When the company confiscates the exclusive right over the final product and blocks parallel developments, it draws a huge profit from the totality of the social efforts that it did not have to finance.

If it's not legitimate, does it at least work? The unique character of knowledge as a factor of production has long been known. A text written by Thomas Jefferson in 1813 is a gem on the subject:

> If nature has made any one thing less susceptible, than all others, of exclusive property, it is the action of the thinking power called an Idea; (...) that ideas should freely spread from one to another over the globe, for the moral and mutual instruction of man, and improvement of his condition, seems to have been peculiarly and benevolently designed by nature, when she made them, like fire, expansible over all space, without lessening their density in any point; and like the air in which we breathe, move, and have our physical being, incapable of confinement, or exclusive appropriation. Inventions then cannot in nature be a subject of property.

Knowledge is not property in the same sense as a physical good. The pen is mine and I do what I want with it. Knowledge, as a result of considerable social efforts, follows another logic. This is why its ownership is not permanently guaranteed. It may last twenty years, in the case of patents, or almost a century, in the case of copyrights, but always for a limited time. Intellectual property is guaranteed for a social purpose – to stimulate people to invent or write – and not as a natural right.

Merit is a central issue to us all, and the main presentation of the feeble fairy tale that we have been told. According to the authors, "nothing is more deeply held among ordinary people than the idea that a person is entitled to what he creates or his efforts produce" (96). In fact, the creators are not the ones who get paid, but instead the legal, financial, and commercial communications intermediaries, who take over the results of creativity, locking them in exclusivity contracts and making fortunes with arguable merit. It is not creativity that is compensated, but the appropriation of the results: "If much of what we have comes to us as the free gift of many generations of historical contribution, there is a profound question as to how much can reasonably be said to be 'earned' by any one person, now or in the future" (97).

People generally fail to realize the limitations. Today, 95% of the maize planted in the US is a single variety. Genetic diversity is disappearing and the menace to our future is significant. Paulo Freire's work will only be available on open access in 2067, 90 years after the author's death. Villa-Lobos' work will become available in 2034. Whose creativity is this helping? Twenty-year patents may have seemed reasonable half a century ago, but with today's rhythm of innovations, what sense does this make? Twenty-five million people have already died from AIDS, while pharmaceutical companies (the Big Pharma) sit on endless patents to antiretroviral medication, blocking access in the countries affected by the disease. That is, the top of the pyramid is increasing its wealth not because of their contributions, but because they have appropriated the result of the accumulation of successive generations, different institutions. These are contributions from the educational system, public and private research centers, universities, and many others.[15]

In this era, in which the wealth concentration is becoming unsustainable, understanding the mechanisms of wealth generation and appropriation is central. The authors are not extremists at all, but they defend that access to the results of productive efforts should be at least in part proportional to the contributions. "The most important source of modern prosperity is societal wealth in the form of cumulative knowledge and inherited technology", which means that "a substantial portion of current wealth and income should be reallocated to all members of society equally or, at a minimum, to promote greater equality" (153). If it weren't for the invention of transistors and semiconductors as well as the logic systems developed during World War II, a person like Bill Gates would still be playing with cathode tubes in his garage. Production is more social than ever and appropriation is more private than ever. Sounds familiar?

The ideological tale: the narrative of merit

Systems must create the ideological excuse for their existence. Exploitation, that is, the appropriation of the social surplus by a minority, searches for a reasonable explanation, a narrative as we call it today, even if it is untruthful. The organized superstructure of power will strive to form a self-sustainable and cohesive system. This will usually combine two elements. First, a mechanism for extracting social wealth paired with an ideological construction to explain exploitation as some type of merit of the upper classes. This will justify their appropriation of a third party's labor (slaves,

[15] Mariana Mazzucato provides many examples in her excellent *The Entrepreneurial State,* Anthem Press, 2013.

serfs, wage earners, or even outsourced workers, depending on the time and region). Second, a police and military force, used in the name of order and the safety of the people.

The "narratives" are not something new. Africans could be enslaved because they had no soul; serfs had to obey because the king was chosen by God, and feudal lords had blue blood; wage-earners had to survive on what they earned because the rich were richer due to their own merit. To each situation, there is a corresponding, and frequently primitive, fairy tale, sufficiently repeated by those who control and shape the public opinion to "catch on" and become common sense. How is it that we believed, for centuries, in the "blue blood" and "divine right to the throne" fairy tale? How easily we assume as the truth whatever satisfies us, despite the utter nonsense it may be! As long as it satisfies our deep-rooted prejudices, it is enough. The process grows in scale when a mass of people is willing to believe in the same babble. Collective stupidity plagues humanity. Barbara Tuchman's classic *The march of folly* is a wonderful piece of writing on the subject.

> Wooden-headedness, the source of self-deception, is a factor that plays a remarkably large role in government. It consists of assessing a situation in terms of preconceived fixed notions while ignoring or rejecting any contrary signs. It is acting according to wish while not allowing oneself to be deflected by the facts. (8) *Homo sapiens*?

Systems change, technologies evolve, but the scheme remains the same. In the current stage of the knowledge economy, the troublesome subject of the legitimacy of knowledge ownership comes forth. The change is radical in relation to the previous systems: the land belongs to one or another, machines have owners; these are "rival" goods. In the case of knowledge, as we saw, use does not deplete stock. If we share knowledge, we still keep it, no loss suffered. And, since knowledge generates more knowledge once transmitted, it's a win-win situation. Therefore, the tendency towards the free dissemination of knowledge has, for the better, become strong. This urges oligarchies to create, besides new mechanisms for social surplus extraction, a new fairy tale, a narrative that will be greatly reinforced by the truncheon of the security forces, in case some stubborn individuals choose to believe otherwise.

These are the three pillars of our social organization: a mechanism for surplus extraction; a fairy tale, elegantly called a "narrative"; and a truncheon for the skeptic. The relative weight of each subsystem of power changes according to circumstances. People understand perfectly well the truncheon's role. They understand much less about the origin of the fairy tale, and next to nothing about the economic mechanisms. Those who wish to clarify or transform the economic mechanisms and those who refuse the fairy tale are the first to take the blow. Ghandi, Mandela and Lula are, in a way, cellmates.

The different modes of production – slavery, feudalism or capitalism – have created, with these three elements, their own systemic logic, guaranteeing their survival for centuries. But when the economic mechanisms change at the productive base of society, the whole edifice is shaken. The nobility danced in Versailles, told the poor to eat *brioche* since they had no bread, without realizing they were standing in a luxurious and artificial limbo, with the ground rapidly vanishing beneath their feet. This text and the arguments we bring together here come from the perception that the economic mechanisms and productive base have changed, and that, even if some simulacra of the democratic phase and competitive capitalism remain, the times have changed. There are certain similarities between Versailles and Davos.

The main narrative of industrial capitalism was simple: as rich people become richer, their wealth is converted into factories, and thus jobs, products, and taxes. Money in the hands of the poor is bound to become unproductive consumption. The great transformation is that, in the current capitalism, where wealth comes by means of the financial "snowball", capitalism has itself become unproductive: it hinders the productive capacity instead of boosting it. The capitalism of the "no capital" era is in search of a narrative to justify the escalating wealth concentration and the fact that the wealthy are unproductive barriers to productivity. In this sense, the enormous power of the informational/financial system is extremely fragile. The hatred spreading across the world against exploitative financial systems and virtual control systems is visibly connected to the fact that people are starting to understand how dysfunctional the system is and how they have been deceived. The narrative of the industrial era simply does not work anymore in the context of the rentists' unproductive wealth accumulation. What still protects the system is, curiously enough, the population's difficulty to understand the financial systems.[16]

---

[16] Thomas Piketty's last book, *Capital et Idéologie*, is a masterful description of the different "narratives", or fairy tales, created to justify inequality. The final part of the book presents a set of measures to bring us down to earth.

For the emerging mode of production, controlling the financial flows and communication and information media is more important than controlling the traditional means of production. The priority is taking over the mechanisms for changing laws by controlling parliaments and judiciary branches; buying universities and research institutions and everything related to knowledge production; creating information and communication platforms to gain control over even people's intimacy. The economic mechanisms have changed and are still changing rapidly. The truncheon blows are being dealt and the corresponding fairy tale is still searching for an acceptable argument. How can an immense wealth concentration in the hands of unproductive groups be justified? Or the destructive appropriation of natural resources that harm future generations? In the feudal system, there was at least the justification that the nobleman's castle would protect the serfs in times of war. The barons of the financial system offer what in return for their extractions? The Washington Consensus increasingly resembles the pact of the nobility of the 1815 Congress of Vienna. The elites have always tended to blindly believe their privileges were legitimate or at least in their ability to create an adequate fairy tale in their defense.

The narrowing spaces of personal freedom

I tend to follow Streeck's view that, in a way, the emerging animal does not fit into the scope of democracy. It may even coexist with elections, for sure, but to what point does voting make sense nowadays? Considering people don't believe in its utility anymore, and the subsystems that organize society's participation and basic democratic mechanisms are being dismantled? What effective instrument for representation do the Democratic and Republican parties constitute? What remains of the Unions, fragmented to the same extent that the whole working class is fragmented and disconnected in different professions and levels? What remains of the citizen-based organizations, persecuted and restricted on all sides? The non-organized masses have no effective controlling power. They may even be hundreds of millions of unsatisfied people, but an organized and articulated minority will exert a much stronger power: this is the penetration power of specific interests in opposition to the diffuse interests of the majority. Naomi Klein presents an excellent description of the minorities in power's ability to cause a rupture, both in *The shock doctrine* and in the more recent *No is not enough*.

Furthermore, the new technologies open the way for individualized control. This ability is growing at an impressive speed. Privacy invasion is now overwhelming, and people are mostly uninformed or indifferent. Who will be interested in monitoring what happens in our monotonous daily life? The truth is there is much interest in it. The regular person will discover the impact of this appropriation of their personal information by various systems when they go job hunting, or hire insurance, or open an account, when they buy an item in installments, or apply for a visa, hire health insurance, or try to protect themselves from online attacks and cyberbullying. Our detailed information – name, address, pictures, and intimate details – in the hands of powerful institutions or simply irresponsible people and numerous commercial, religious, or ideological groups, can deeply affect our lives, both individually and collectively.

The first issue is that technologies have made privacy invasion simple and cheap. In the computing era, obtaining detailed and individualized information on millions of people presents no technical difficulty. Algorithms make it possible to treat and cross data, making it easy for interested agents, whether governments, companies, or criminal organizations, to individualize the information and focus on a single person, family, group of workers in a company, group of individuals with a specific illness, and so on.

Privacy invasion can equally have a strategic character in politics and economics. The NSA having recorded private conversations between Angela Merkel and Dilma Rousseff constitutes an international political instrument, including the fact that they passed this information on to other interested institutions in other countries. An institution like Cambridge Analytica playing around with Facebook data to alter elections has become a common thing. The access to internal conversations from governments before international meetings, to become familiar with the upcoming proposals, is a strategic advantage that caused protests in countries in the European Union.

Invading Petrobrás computers to gain access to confidential information about Pre-Sal reserves – which was made easier with the pretext of fighting corruption – is a form of political and industrial espionage with evident impact. This is in the immediate interests of international groups of the sector. It is not only a question of individual and personal privacy. A private company such as Serasa Experian decides to control our financial life, just as companies like Fitch, Moody's and Standard & Poor feel entitled to evaluate our governments' trustworthiness. Did someone elect them? Is there any equivalent instrument to control the financial systems themselves?

Behind this rapid transformation process, naturally, is technology. The advances are impressive, and the rhythm of transformations radically exceeds the slow-paced advances in the legislation, regulations, and cultural changes themselves. Envelopes could be closed and sealed, dossiers could be stored in vaults, the doors to a meeting could be locked, intimate pictures or family pictures were kept in the peace of photo albums. Today these are all magnetic signals, immaterial information that can be accessed anywhere, stored and treated with Big Data technology, analyzed with algorithms, transmitted worldwide in instants.

The process is deeply asymmetrical. As individuals, we are radically vulnerable. But the system is managed by giants. In the governmental levels, these are, for instance, the NSA and the GCHQ. The world's essential information flows through them. There are also the information giants, like Alphabet (Google), Facebook, Microsoft, Apple, Amazon, Verizon, and only a few others. All of them simply won't allow us to access either the vast amounts of information they gather or the decisions about how to use it. With the exception of the rare heroic leaks, like the files revealed by Edward Snowden or the initiatives of Julian Assange, the population has no idea what happens to their information. In actual terms, we are impotent. The truth is we are rapidly advancing towards a type of Big Brother world, in which the corporations' power associated with the State's power radically changes the concept of citizen. Obtaining the submission of the populations will become progressively easier, as algorithms gain the ability to identify nonconformist individuals and groups with much anticipation. The truncheon can be kept for extreme cases. But for the majority, the conformism generated through diffuse control and the fairy tale will be sufficient.[17]

We are witnessing a transformation of the superstructures as a whole, in the forms of organization of power that are slowly catching up with the profound changes in the productive base. The time of capitalism with democracy, elections and citizens is becoming farther and farther away and less important. The superstructures being created are different.

---

[17] Basic reading on this issue is obviously *The Age of Surveillance Capitalism* by Shoshana Zuboff, Public Affairs, New York, 2019: "Surveillance capitalism is a boundary-less form that ignores older distinctions between market and society, market and world, or market and person. It is a profit-seeking form in which production is subordinated to extraction as surveillance capitalists unilaterally claim control over human, societal, and political territories extending far beyond the conventional institutional terrain of the private firm or the market." (514)

***

The superstructures of power, the inherited rules of the game – the worker receiving what corresponds to his workforce and the capitalist receiving the results of his capital – suggest the system is fair and productive. They are clearly losing legitimacy in the new context. Governments connected to corporations resort to increasingly fewer democratic means to balance a system that was forced to halt. The gap between the economic base of the 21st century and the rules of the game inherited from the past centuries is growing. This is a systemic gap, not very different from the one that affected the superstructure of the feudal system, as it progressively lost balance with an economic base that was evolving into the era of manufacturing and industrial capitalism.

With all its power, and despite the search for new systemic coherence, the new organization has a basic weakness: the wealth accumulation at the top of the pyramid is visibly unproductive, and the narrative of merit is rapidly dwindling. Especially in economic terms, the system takes over the surplus not by producing or stimulating production but on the contrary by generating scarcity. The high concentration of income and wealth increases inequality. Today, the poor are aware they are being massacred. And the poor are many. The forms of production are an environmental disaster, and people around the world are starting to take action. In terms of social, environmental, and economic functioning, the system is becoming more and more dysfunctional. The opportunities arise, naturally, from necessity and from the possibility of reverting the setbacks, tensions, and insecurity in the world. The social sacrifices and social, economic, and political dramas that we suffer are simply unnecessary. Folly, Barbara Tuchman would say.

It is essential to better understand what is emerging, what are the necessary transformations in the rules of the game for the rising society – with its two major axes, the knowledge economy and the financial system – to adopt a more adequate set of rules and political system. For the time being, we are far from this. What we have are fierce laws of private property protection, while the economy's main factor of production, knowledge, could be spread across all of society. Also, central banks have no power to control the global system of virtual currency; private banks are the ones that issue and control financial resources. The result is generalized rentism, without the corresponding productive contribution. And national governments have lost strength; the globalized financial economy escapes their control. With the title *Rewriting the Rules*, Stiglitz is opening the way, in his discussion on the current system, for a much broader revision of how we organize ourselves as a society. Martin Wolf, the chief economist of the Financial Times, rightly concludes that "the system has lost its legitimacy". But the oppressive system that is rising may expand in proportion to its lack of legitimacy.

IV –

THE RISING OPPORTUNITIES

At the center of the ongoing transformations – in the sense of the results of the dynamics of the economy, not the outlines of an ideal society – is the fact we spoke of exhaustively earlier in this study: the main factor of production can be used without reducing stocks. As an immaterial factor of production, knowledge may be stored, analyzed, transmitted, and disseminated without constraints at practically zero cost. This immaterial factor, sent by electromagnetic waves, may be disseminated to the entire population and all companies through simple and cheap pocket-sized equipment.

All the knowledge accumulated by humanity is available somewhere, except that corporations hinder access, claiming the legitimacy of intellectual property. We can't ignore the immense generalization of prosperity within the bounds of possibility, just as we can't ignore the war waged by corporations and rentists to block access. The capitalism of the corporate giants, who extract wealth instead of guaranteeing its wider access, has a weak spot. Epstein and Montecino, from the Roosevelt Institute, keenly remark this is "negative net productivity".

The fact that we may spread knowledge across the world, granting access to all, regardless of income levels, with no additional costs, in terms of organization of the economic basis of the 21st century, has a huge impact. We live in the open-access era, that is, the era of the potential of open access. The institutions responsible for blocking access and generating artificial scarcity are increasingly becoming visible for what they are: barriers to the socialization of progress. The concept of property and in particular its legitimacy must be radically reviewed. Not for philosophical or legal reasons but for the sake of society's systemic productivity.

To unblock our ability to spread progress and prosperity, it is fundamental that we also recover the right to take back control of our financial resources. These resources are now also part of the immaterial economy; a set of magnetic signals which are means and not ends. When Germans put their savings in the *Sparrkassen* – savings banks in their cities and communities

– and use these savings to develop their region, their savings become productive again, instead of contributing to speculation and tax havens if they were put in banks. The issue here is the concept of unearned income: what we know as rentism and associate to people who "live off investments". These are frequently charming characters, well portrayed in early 20th-century literature on the leisure-class. Today, they drain our productive potential.

These two alternative paths – generalizing open access and redirecting resources to finance the necessary initiatives – are leading us to radically rethink economics, a social science with which we can systematize an important, albeit insufficient, dimension of a functioning world. Access to knowledge and resources is vital for people and groups across the world to move towards the progress of their communities. Big capital controls knowledge and financial resources. For access to the first, they charge royalties, patents, and copyrights. For access to the latter, they charge monstrous interest rates and demand extorsive dividends. A minority of privileged rich expand their fortunes by hampering development rather than promoting it.

We know quite well what must be done: the Sustainable Development Goals (2030 Agenda) are an excellent systematization of priorities such as reducing inequality and poverty. They are broadly directed towards economically viable, socially just, and environmentally sustainable societies. Widespread access to knowledge in the broad sense and access to financial resources are the basic means for these goals to become a reality. As a society, we hold all the aces, but they are in the wrong hands.

Open Access

Let's return to the main systemic change: as the land stood for the agrarian era and the machine for the industrial era, with their respective arrangements of property, governments, and ideology, now, knowledge is the main factor defining a new mode of production. Financial resources are not a factor of production *per se*. Issuing copious amounts of currency does not add to a country's wealth, but provides an instrument for appropriating productive resources that should be directed to those who best incentivize the real economy. The war to control knowledge – and the financial resources that enable appropriating knowledge – is behind the different access regulations and "fairy-tales", or "narratives", that dominate the new economic, social, and cultural fields. Knowledge and financial resources are both immaterial.

The difference is that one is the main factor of production while the other is only the means.

The immateriality of the main factor of production is the central transformation. Knowledge may be accessed from a device that any person has, or will soon have, on their desks or in their pockets. Knowledge may be reproduced, retransmitted, and appropriated by any person, company, or institution with no additional costs. It has immense potential for generating technological advances and innovation, benefiting those from researchers to small farmers. While Rousseau accredited a great part of our misfortunes to the first man to point to a patch of land and declare "this is mine", today we have an enormous opportunity for creating a collaborative society and shared prosperity. The new Rousseaunian man would point to the factor of production that today is collectively produced and say: "This is ours".

Regarding patents, Stiglitz and Greenwald present the problem in its contemporary dimension, referring to patent thickets:

> Anybody engaged in writing a software program, for instance, even doing so with complete originality, faces the risk that in doing so she may have trespassed on one of hundreds of thousands of related software patents or that she may have come close enough to trespassing to make herself libel to litigation. No one can keep up with the myriad of patents being issued – if one did, it would be difficult to have time to engage in research. In this sense, the patent system itself has become a roadblock to innovation. (Stiglitz and Greenwald, 434)

Michael Heller, cited by the authors, uses a suggestive name to denounce this distortion: the *anticommons*.

Among the most notable contributions along these lines is Elinor Orstom and Charlotte Hess's work, *Understanding Knowledge as a Commons*: "*Commons* became a buzzword for digital information, which was being enclosed, commodified, and overpatented. Whether labeled the 'digital', 'electronic', 'information', 'virtual', 'communication', 'intellectual', 'Internet', or 'technological' commons, all these concepts address the new shared territory of global distributed information" (4). This new territory is characterized by its enormous potential for collective appropriation: "the more people who share useful knowledge, the greater the common good. Consideration of knowledge as a commons, therefore, suggests that the unifying thread in all commons resources is that they are jointly used, managed by groups of varying sizes and interests" (5).

Elinor Ostrom dedicated her life as a researcher to common goods like water, forests, fishing resources, and others. Her work earned her the Nobel Prize from the Bank of Sweden, by the way, the first Nobel in Economics awarded to a woman. Together with Charlotte Hess, she organized a collection in which she used her previous studies on common goods to consider the role of knowledge and include it among the "commons". She brought together important authors. The chapters were shared among all of them, so they refer to each other: it is a construction and analysis of the challenges presented by the profound transformation that characterizes the 21st century.

Open access does not mean a lack of management, an "anything goes" situation. It implies adequate rules to value the commons through innovative institutional arrangements. The chapters present the views of, among other authors: James Boyle, on information as an ecosystem, calling attention to the absurdity of blocking open access to works for more than seventy years (125); Wendy Lougee, on the transformations of the university and particularly the roles of university libraries in the context of universally available knowledge; Peter Suber, on the evolution of open access; Shubha Gosh, on the new concepts of intellectual property; Nancy Kranich, on the corporations' attempts to block access and generate a new "enclosures" movement; and Peter Levine, on the forms of organization of civil society in the new arrangements.

The most basic rule is the following: to a company in the pharmaceutical sector, for instance, blocking access to an active ingredient is advantageous, but the company's profit is incomparably smaller than the loss to society in terms of the multiplying effects this piece of knowledge could have. Knowledge production itself happens in the Remix, so well identified by Lawrence Lessig, of numerous technological advances in society. It is a question of unblocking access, liberating knowledge, opening the road tolls to creativity. Between investing in research and losing global systemic productivity due to these access tolls, there is an extreme imbalance. When the MIT decided to provide open access to its research (OCW), resulting in millions of texts downloaded worldwide, it transformed public investments on research into numerous innovations from other public or private institutions, with a multiplying effect on general productivity.

Connectivity and the network society

Since the initial works of Manuel Castells on the network society, the process has intensified and the studies on the new tendencies have multiplied. What type of democratic governance is possible, when national governments are losing space and corporate giants are becoming global powers? There is no global government to counter the power of corporations, or any political power capable of doing so. David Held provides a good summary of the issue:

> What is noteworthy about the modern global system is the stretching of social relations in and through new dimensions of activity and the chronic intensification of patterns of interconnectedness mediated by such phenomena as modern communication networks and new information technology. (…) The balance of power has shifted in favor of capital *vis-à-vis* both national governments and national labor movements. As a result, the autonomy of democratically elected governments has been, and is increasingly constrained by sources of unelected and unrepresentative economic power. (David Held, *Democracy and Globalization,* in Archibugi, 13, 18)

The extent of the change is directly connected to global connectivity, which makes it possible for a group headquartered in Geneva, London, or New York to operate thousands of companies across the planet, an authentic *Telemanagement*, a remote management system, deepening the economic and environmental imbalances. On the plus side, the same connectivity allows productive units, individuals or companies, university professors or small startups, to create partnerships with people or organizations with similar or complementary goals, wherever they may physically be located. Today any clinic or civil society organization multiplies their connections, technology exchanges, and other forms of collaboration worldwide by weaving a global network of interdependencies that passes over a large number of regulations and bureaucratic complexities since immaterial input is only symbolically controlled. The same social-technical basis that enables corporate control opens space for decentralized creative production networks.

Today, this connectivity could open the way, for instance, for a basic income to poor families in any part of the world, as was done with millions of people in Brazil; or for an accurate focus on millions of HIV-positive people, reducing the spread and systemic costs of the illness; or for organizing with precision reforestation programs in regions threatened by desertification; or controlling in detail pollution and contamination sources. In other words, we are taking the first steps towards the immense potential that this ample transformation has opened: the evolution into an immaterial economy; the global connectivity that permits decentralized management through networks; and virtual money that can free us from the enormous tolls we pay to those who neither contribute, nor even own the money they lend.

The corporate giants have made use of the technological advances to extend longer tentacles and control segments of the economy and even politics throughout the world. But the same tools are opening the possibility of expanding horizontal collaboration networks. Between one use and the other, there is no doubt the corporations are winning the game. They were the first to finance the appropriation of technology and turn it in their favor. But new dynamics are emerging everywhere. Jeremy Rifkin is among those who realized the extent of the transformation:

> The market economy is far too slow to take full advantage of the speed and productive potential made possible by the software and communications revolutions. The result is that we are witnessing the birth of a new economic system that is as different from market capitalism as the latter was from the feudal economy of an earlier era. (537)

The truth is that the monumental and costly pyramids of bureaucratic power that corporations have become have a major weak spot: they have a negative systemic impact both in environmental and social terms. And, especially, in economic terms: have you already checked your mobile bills? Do you think they are proportionate to the costs of the service offered to you by the telecom operator? Do the electromagnetic waves that cross the planet suddenly have an owner? The collaborative economy is opening a new space here, even if only with the first steps.

The collaborative potential

If I can give someone something valuable and still keep it myself, as in the case of an immaterial idea, the concept of competition radically shifts. Arun Sundararajan's *The Sharing Economy* is one of the best comprehensive analyses on the subject of the title, as indispensable as Jeremy Rifkin's *The zero marginal cost society* to understand the new dynamics. The internet of things is, broadly speaking, a commercial activity that makes use of the ample connectivity between people and economic agents and the intangible nature of the inputs to develop a great variety of organizational architectures. The good thing is that the author makes a clear systematization of the activities; economic, cultural, and legal challenges; impacts on employment; and forms of regulation. The fact that he provides numerous examples and explains them is very helpful.

Sundararajan briefly presents the varieties of this new form of economic organization:

> Our research suggests wide variation across different platforms. Many resemble markets that facilitate entrepreneurship, whereas others look more like hierarchies that employ contractors. Along with Airbnb, Etsy, and BlaBlaCar, labor platforms like Upwork and Thumbtack, social dining platforms like VizEat and Eatwith, the local tour guide exchange platform Vayable (founded by sharing economy pioneer Jamie Wong) are decidedly more market-like, ridesharing platforms Lyft and Uber fall somewhere in between, and focused services or labor platforms like Luxe, Postmates, and Universal Avenue bear a closer resemblance to hierarchies than the average sharing economy platform does. (Sundararajan, 77)

Connectivity is vital here. In the knowledge economy, we transform, through Wikipedia for instance, the knowledge capital sitting in people's heads into social wealth. In the case of the financial system, this same connectivity enables, through appropriate platforms, the removal of intermediaries in credit, putting directly in contact those who have sitting money and those who need it. We are taking the first steps towards the immense opportunities that global connectivity offers us, including technologies like Blockchain. We speak here of underused capital, but also of underused work.

The car is an interesting example. Private cars are used on average one hour a day, only 4% of their transportation potential, and travel with an average of 1.3 passengers, despite having room for 5. In total, we are using about 1% of this capital's capacity, which remains stagnant for hours, parked at workplaces, in home garages, clogging the street parking spots, or just caught up in traffic. Today, we have residential buildings in Sweden where some cars in the garage are the common property of the owners' corporation. People will take whichever one is available.

Paris has had for a while now a network of public electric vehicles, parked across town, as was done initially with bicycles. The user receives an app on their phone indicating where the vehicles can be found or left. These places have battery rechargers. This produces more intensive use and reduces traffic and pollution. In the case of Airbnb, the waste with vacant rooms or houses is equally clear. The principle is the same in general. There are so many things we have or buy that we use only once or a couple of times. The success of tool-sharing platforms shows this.

But the corporate dynamics that give absolute priority to money and short-term goals generate other challenges. In Berlin, for instance, Airbnb was banned. At first, it worked; retired folks or families on vacation could earn some extra money by renting their apartment, for instance. But large real estate groups started buying entire residential buildings to rent for tourists, reducing the available housing for Berliners and making rent prices rise, which led to a crisis. This is the chaotic coexistence of different rationalities; it is the market's "anything goes" in the scope of an economy that has changed in nature. The great economic freedom represented by the fact that anyone with internet access can develop economic activities as a producer and not only a consumer (what is being called the prosumer) can be transformed by corporations into oppressive systems, due to the sheer size and scale of their operations.

As a whole, collaborative initiatives are thriving, since there are clear opportunities and economic advantages for the whole of the economy (and not only for the contractors), given that these initiatives use the existing wealth more efficiently. Some things are quite simple: parking apps reduce the time we spend searching for spots. Someone had to have the idea of creating an adequate platform and that's all.

Alex Stephany, cited by Sundararajan, summarizes the arguments well when he mentions the advantages: 1) easier and less bureaucratic exchanges and payments; 2) activation of stagnant or underutilized assets; (3) online accessibility with the power of the Internet; (4) community strengthening through local exchange systems and initiatives; and (5) a reduced need for ownership, which is substituted by the practicality of access (in Sundararajan, 30).

But we are developing innovative practices in spaces already taken by economic giants. We are facing a legal void that raises fear and natural tension due to the transition and coexistence. Frequently, as in the case of Uber, the strength of the platform is much greater than that of the contractors. Tax payment is still relatively fluid, and between protests and proposals, a new set of rules to the game is being outlined. Simply banning the potential of network connections does not solve the problem. But the "anything goes" mentality of the so-called free market in the face of the new technologies finds a limit.

We have, then, to move beyond the logic of individual advantages as the sole engine of the economy. Regarding collaboration, one of the most prominent scholars of the knowledge society, Lawrence Lessig, suggests that perhaps what is most important is

> you have to give people a sense of being part of something that has meaning. (…) If you look at Wikipedia, for example, people genuinely feel like they're part of something: they're helping to build a repository of human

> knowledge, and that's an amazing thing. It's a full spectrum of motivation, just like you get the full spectrum of motivation in free software. (Lessig, 185)

The creative economy, collaboration networks, the solidarity economy, the sharing principle, and other initiatives bring a fresh breeze to the oppressive corporate system that urges us to buy more things that, in our desperate and ever-lasting search for money, we have less and less time or patience to appreciate. The change is welcome and, in my view, inexorable, despite the traditional corporations' major attempts to halt or absorb innovations. There are challenges ahead of us, issues that generate tension and debate: new technologies create new relations of production, with risks and opportunities, and the rules of this new system are only just starting to take shape.

Demographic transformations

Not many studies have been conducted on the demographic transformations, in terms of their impact on economic and social organization. A central axis of change is urbanization. We are now a dominantly urban global population. In Brazil, 87% of the population lives in cities. This creates a set of opportunities regarding development policies. The present centralized management of the country is not viable for simple reasons related to management mechanisms. We have 5,570 highly diversified cities. Most developed countries today have decentralized management systems; each city has autonomy and resources to manage their policies according to local interests and specificities. This makes management more rational, due to the proximity between decision-making and the impacts on the community. It also makes politics at the national level more rational, since central government can focus on the nation's structural and long-term problems. The current system, with mayors standing in line in the waiting rooms of ministers, doesn't work for either side. The result is a complex architecture of under-the-radar benefits. Despite all the goodwill, politics without a corresponding administrative organization simply does not work.

The idea of getting the best from local abilities, with up-close politics and management, is deeply related to the advances in connectivity and horizontal networks. Today, even smaller or more isolated cities can perfectly well maintain connections with their entire region or with research centers, technological and commercial information sources, and so on. Urban Wi-Fi is progressing across the world, guaranteeing free or nearly free connectivity to all economic and social agents, creating opportunities for small- and medium-sized entrepreneurs, and making it possible to create new connections between cities' rural and urban areas. The Piraí Digital Project is one example among many initiatives of this type. A decentralized, network-based urban management opens space for a new architecture of decision-making, that is more efficient and democratic. When communities participate in the construction and transformation of their surroundings, a very different political atmosphere is created, with less "them" and more "us", what we call empowerment. It carries immense underused opportunities.[18]

A second important demographic axis is the transformation of the family. Traditionally, the nuclear family was part of a process of social reproduction between generations. What we call "home" had at least three generations. The younger, still unproductive children, as well as the productive generation and the elders, all had a place at the table. The intergenerational reproduction was guaranteed by the extended family. Homes now are generally composed of a couple with one or two children, living in a house or apartment, in a neighborhood where neighbors barely know each other. In Brazil, the average number of inhabitants per household is 3.1. Millions of households are made of single mothers with children. In Europe, the average number of people per household is 2.4. When there are enough resources, the elders may live in a nursing home. The family has been transformed into a commercially ideal economic micro-unit, with an apartment, a refrigerator, a television, and a couch. Separations are increasingly frequent. Few couples survive in a world where claustrophobia prevails.

Where there's trouble, there's also opportunity. Many countries have social policies, along the lines of the welfare state, guaranteeing infrastructures and policies that compensate for what nuclear families can't provide. The adult men who dominate politics and the entrepreneurial world combat with outrage what they qualify as the Nanny-State, at least while they are not yet old. But the fact is there are countries and cities systematically organized to shelter with social resources that which individual resources can't account for anymore. This opens an enormous space for an economy of care that must expand, because, also, life expectancy is increasing. Instead of fighting against social security, we must expand our abilities in this area.

The new challenges also create opportunities in terms of community organization; sociability spaces compensate for isolation and individualization.

---

[18] On this subject, see my *O que é Poder Local? (What is Local Power?)*, available online at dowbor.org.

Numerous cities have open spaces – parks, public pools, sports, and leisure centers – distributed in neighborhoods within walking distance for the local community. These cities also have different cultural events that recreate the social tissue damaged by modern urban and family dynamics. We have inherited the idea that we only exist, economically speaking, if we have a job, if we are capable of buying the said apartment, refrigerator, couch, and television. This idea can evolve to a much freer and open mentality of coexistence, where the social economy has a broad reach. The argument that these policies exceed the budget is meant only for the benefit of private companies who wish to take over the spaces of leisure and socialization, with much higher costs and a resulting increase in hierarchical social organization.

Another structural transformation in the same area is the expanding economic and social roles of women, which naturally represent advances not only for women but for the whole of society. We will not pore over the obvious inequality in salaries, employment, political representation, and rights. We will call attention here to the fact that, just as contraceptives gave women the right over their destinies as mothers, the evolution from the industrial society to the knowledge society opens radically new perspectives in terms of how society is managed. Men's muscular advantage is becoming less significant in the modern economy. Today, approximately 57% of higher education graduates are women and 43% men, and this difference tends to grow. The fact that the modern economy is increasingly anchored on knowledge deeply changes the outlines of our social future. The alpha males who dominate us, with their explosive egos, in positions of authority in politics and corporations, are part of the last century. They reproduce a society of unsustainable violence, inequality, and discrimination. A more balanced society in terms of gender tends to be simply more civilized.

Urbanization, changes in family structure and social organization, women's growing participation, and the knowledge economy tend to outline new ways of living. The civil society organizations will have a much more prominent role in the scope of less centralized and more participative politics. These are not dreams, they are underutilized potentials. The economy can move towards activities that enrich our daily lives. It is not centered only on what we can buy anymore.

The potential of social policies

A set of opportunities arises from the changes in the intersectoral composition of our activities. When we talk about economic activity, we tend to refer to manufacturing, agriculture, construction, and the like. But it is important to keep in mind that agriculture, for instance, represents approximately 3% of the United States' economy; manufacturing as a whole, a little over 10%, and it is decreasing; while the health sector alone represents 20% of the GDP, and it is growing. In other words, what we understand as economic activities has deeply changed.

People tend to sum up the change as the weight of the so-called services. In scientific terms, this is a disaster since, as Manuel Castells says, "services" is a residual concept: we know what agriculture is and that it is connected to the land. And we know what manufacturing is and that it is organized in factories. In general terms, all the "rest" is what we call services. When the "rest", the "others", corresponds to three-quarters or more of what we analyzed, we obviously have a methodological problem. Labeling three-quarters of our activities as "services" does not answer anything. But when we unfold "services", a concept that deserves to be stored away, and distinguish its components, we can have a useful understanding of the situation.

On the one hand, we have the gigantism of the intermediary systems, particularly the commercial and financial ones. In the United States, for some decades now, the financial intermediaries had taken over 10% of the country's corporate profit. Today, they appropriate more than 40%. The commercial intermediaries, especially the giants known as traders, have also become heavy-weight players in the social surplus appropriation: only 16 groups control the majority of the world's commodity trade. We may call this sector of activities "intermediation services"; it has an internal coherence of its own and must be analyzed so we may understand the world's economic distortion. Financial, commercial, and legal intermediaries now take over social products much more than producers themselves.

On the other hand, we have the enormous sector we broadly call the social policies: health, education, sports, leisure, culture, security, and others. They are fundamentally productive activities, since they are investments in people, and also indispensable to our quality of life. We all want a healthy, culturally rich life, with security and other similar conditions. Contrary to intermediation activities, which are means, this sector reflects what we want from life, the end activities.

The general goal of the economy is, or should be, the well-being of families, which must be sustainably assured, that is, without destroying our children's futures. Well-being is not limited to a base salary, to the income we earn.

Income has an essential role, without doubt. It lets us buy stuff, or pay rent. But almost equally important is what we call indirect salary, the access to collective consumption that becomes possible when a country has public health, education, culture, security, an environment without pollution, and other similar provisions.

Canadians, to give an example, have lower wages in comparison to North Americans, but they have free daycare in their neighborhoods, schools with sports infrastructure, green streets that improve quality of life, and so on. It is worth noting that Canada guarantees public, free, and universal access to health services, with excellent results and an average annual disbursement of 4.4 thousand dollars per person, while the average American spends – from their own pocket, as a regular commercial transaction – an average 10.4 thousand dollars every year on healthcare. The OCDE evaluates that the United States has the most ineffective health system among the developed countries. The British citizen's health costs 4 thousand dollars a year, with a significantly superior level. Indirect salary works. Privatized healthcare is a terrible business.

The well-being of families also depends on investments in infrastructure. This goes from paved streets to available clean rivers for leisure, efficient transportation systems, access to safe water, electricity, and even to free broadband. This last facility is already guaranteed as a public service in many cities across the world. The important thing here is that these three dynamics, essential for living with dignity – direct income for everyday expenses, access to collective consumer goods and infrastructure to make a balanced everyday life possible, and adequate environmental conditions – depend only partially on the private sector.

Access to income, to "pocket-money", largely depends, without a doubt, on access to employment and a salary, but for those who have retired, who are not capable of working anymore or who cannot find a job, access to income depends on monetary transfers from the public system. When it functions properly, access to basic social services is essentially public, free, and universally guaranteed; this is true for South Korea, China, Germany, Finland, or Canada. We say free, but the system is, naturally, indirectly paid by our taxes. These services are also indirect salary. The result from so many analyses of the productivity of social policies is that they are much more efficient when they are public, universally assured and free of charge. Whenever profit-oriented companies take the place of social policies, we find education for the rich and education for the poor, health for the rich and health for the poor, and all the resulting tensions and losses in systemic productivity.

What matters is that the time when the majority of the population depended solely on pocket money, wages, or other sources of income is gone. Public policies, in any functioning society, represent, to put it in scale, 40% of the economy. Not because populations enjoy the “Nanny State”, as Americans say with contempt, but because it is more efficient in terms of a simple cost-benefit analysis, and because it guarantees more social equality. In the field of social policies, which has acquired more weight than manufacturing and agriculture put together, market mechanisms don’t work. Instead, this is the field of public policies.

Whenever social policies are taken over by companies, instead of smart policies in terms of economic, social, and environmental goals, the result is the sickness industry, the diploma industry, and the impoverishment of culture. In the security sector, what should be the fight against poverty becomes the fight against the poor. But the exponentially growing field of social policies can be a powerful foundation for decentralized and participative forms of economic and social organization: this is where the civil society organizations are mainly situated. The average Swede participates in four community organizations. Social control is vital for the system to work. As connectivity increases due to urbanization and it becomes easier to establish connections and organize participative systems, a much more decentralized and participative governance becomes viable. The low efficiency and efficacy of private systems when it comes to social policies open the way for political and social change.

Access to financial resources

The indebtedness of families, companies, and governments reached the mark of 164 trillion dollars in 2018, more than twice the world GDP. The interest rates charged on these resources drain the capacity of increasing family demands, company production, and government funding of infrastructure and public policies. Dividend extraction has also soared. In Brazil, as we saw earlier, the rentists’ extraction of resources has reached levels that paralyze the economy. In reality, as in the 2008 crisis, the process affects the global economy. Exploitation through indebtedness has become the main source of social surplus appropriation by those who do not produce. And, as the State itself increasingly joins forces with surplus extraction instead of regulating it, the trap starts to involve the entire system.

Zygmunt Bauman analyzes the "parasitic capitalism" in a spirited tone: the current system is a

> success in transforming a huge majority of men and women, old and young, into a race of debtors (…) Capitalism, to put it bluntly, is essentially a parasitic system. Like all parasites, it may thrive for a time once it finds an as yet unexploited organism on which it can feed, but it can't do that without harming the host and sooner or later destroying thereby the conditions of its prosperity, or even of its own survival. (Bauman, 8 and 18)

A permanent drain is formed as debtors become trapped in an endless flow of interests, a debt burden that is much larger than the credit's productive contribution. Financial intermediaries actually hate the good payers. The good clients are those who, time after time, refinance their debts and become a permanent source of supply for the system. "The client who readily pays for the money they borrowed is the creditors' nightmare" (14).

In Brazil, people are starting to realize the absurdity of depositing money in banks that pay them a sum that barely covers the inflation and, when they need resources, – which are not the bank's property – they must pay astronomical interest rates. Usury and abusive money lending are pre-historic practices; with electronic money, they become a global system. Even the humblest contribute to banks, with each purchase on credit cards, and each remittance to their families (an average 7% for these remittances). However, the same capillary nature of the virtual system can promote the inversion of the process. In other words, we must find, in the same technological transformations, the base for our liberation from the permanent draining to which we are submitted, a toll that is both useless and counterproductive.

Do we need these intermediaries? We have alternatives such as cooperative banks (Poland), community development banks (already 115 in Brazil), local public savings banks (Germany's *Sparrkassen*), local currencies (The *Palma*, the *Sampaio* and so many others in Brazil), local public banks (North Dakota, USA), credit NGOs (France's *Placements Ethiques*), direct, intermediary-free contact between producers and clients (family agriculture in Kenya), and even the more radical removal of intermediaries with virtual coins and commercial trade through blockchain technology. All this is still very incipient, but who said virtual money can't be directly exchanged between those who use it productively, without so much intermediation?

The existing banks could then return to the initial reason for their creation: gathering savings for loans, with regulated terms and interest rates. And, in this way, they would help to develop productive activities, generating employment and income. Identifying good investments, evaluating projects, and supervising their execution, in other words, fomenting and providing technical support for the real economy are, naturally, hard work and should receive a fair remuneration. This technical work, centered on the economy's systemic productivity, is necessary. By determining an investment project's financial viability, it is possible to identify, perfectly well, the adequate interest rates that will guarantee the viability of the enterprise. Instead of focusing on publicity, fraud, and usury, they should do their work of contributing to the economy like any other sector of activities.

It is particularly important to understand that financial resources are just magnetic signals and that financial flows must be part of an economic policy for directing these resources to where they will be more productive. And we know how to do this. We have enough experience with cooperative banks, community development banks, micro-credit systems, city savings banks, local currencies, and non-monetary trade systems to recover the utility of money and credit and redirect the use of our resources.

When we direct resources to the base of society, to the families that transform their income into consumption, we increase the demand for goods and services. This demand leads to an expansion of productive activities by the entrepreneurial sector. Both consumption and entrepreneurial activities generate revenue for the State; the first through taxes on consumption, and the latter through taxes on production. This is a means for the State to recover what it initially invested in the base of the economy, covering the initial deficit and expanding the State's ability to amplify the dynamics with investments in infrastructure and social policies. Social policies in the fields of health, education, culture, and security, among others, are investments in people. They guarantee collective consumption, which improves the well-being of families and makes the economy as a whole more productive. The activities of teachers, doctors, and security agents are jobs and necessary products, not "expenditures".

Another economic-financial cycle is produced, in which families' access to consumer goods and collective consumption is improved, the market is expanded for companies to act, unemployment is reduced through the general expansion in activities, and the State recovers its financial balance through the corresponding taxes. This is the "virtuous cycle". It worked in the United States to counter the 1929 crisis (the New Deal). Then, significant taxes on financial fortunes were established (up to 90%) and social policies and redistributive processes were expanded. It worked in

Europe to reconstruct the continent in the post-war period (the Welfare State) when the purchasing power of popular segments of society was systematically increased, salaries were increased proportional to the increase in productivity, and social policies such as health, education, security, and others were expanded, based on principles of universal, public, and free access. It worked in the reconstruction of South Korea, which succeeded in keeping inequality levels extremely low. It works today in China, which has prioritized the expansion of popular consumption and State investments in infrastructure and social policies. It worked, of course, in Brazil between 2003 and 2013, when the reaction from the financial interests had not yet broken the system. We know perfectly well what works in economic terms, even in different political regimes.

What we don't know is how to reconcile the model that functions with the interests of the dominant financial groups in extracting more than they contribute to the economy and even more than the economy can withstand. We have a 21st-century financial system, with virtual currencies and global flows, controlled by financial giants, but we have the laws and forms of economic organization of the last century, inherited from the industrial era. Do we still believe that more money in the hands of the rich will generate more productive investments, jobs, and products? The sole result will be more financial fortunes and the continued drama of the 1% that hold more wealth than the other 99%. The narrative that pushes us on, that the rich know better how to incentivize the economy, is not working anymore. People are not buying it.

***

We presented here some opportunities that arise with the era of knowledge and the intangible economy. The same technological advances that subject us to these giants (GAFAM or BAT) open space for horizontal networks.[19] The virtual currency and generalized connectivity between people and productive companies make it possible to remove the intermediaries and make finance productive and cheap. The network society that Manuel Castells so well describes makes horizontal decision-making in networks viable. The role of authoritarian vertical structures is being minimized. Connectivity, together with intelligent search systems, enables a radical amplification of the forms of collaborative production, an area in which we are taking the first steps. The global ascension of social policies as the main

---

[19] Google, Apple, Facebook, Amazon, Microsoft; Baidu, Alibaba, Tencent – see Douglas Heaven's article in *New Scientist*, 2018.

field of human activity points towards different dynamics, in terms of the expansion of the public sector, civil society organizations, and decentralized and participative forms of management.

These are new settings and opportunities, but until now, what we have seen is privacy invasion and social control by the giants of commercial media; unleashed exploitation through indebtedness and dividend payment; and corporate power pyramids that not only remain unregulated by governments but control political processes. Connectivity enables corporate giants to stretch their tentacles farther. The private appropriation of public policies leads to the growth of harmful forms of rentism in vital areas such as health, education, and security. Thus, we have a world marked by technological advances and uncertain new balances. We could be either heading towards Orwell's Big Brother or more open, democratic, and participative societies. For now, the corporate world is clearly winning the game. Our problem is not a lack of resources, but the ability to use them intelligently. We have more powerful technologies, but the motivations are increasingly doubtful and the aims are simply disastrous.

We have a growing conflict between the diffuse interests of society and the narrow interests of corporations. If the Brazilian population's opinion about the need to preserve the Amazonian rainforest were assessed, the result would surely be almost unanimous. However, this dispersed and fragmented interest is impotent, even if it represents millions of people, in the face of a corporation that sees an opportunity for making millions of dollars by exploiting mahogany, for example. The corporation will know how to finance politicians and judges, or control authorities until they are benefitted. Focused power has much more penetration strength than general interest. We all want to preserve the oceans, but between the diffuse interest of the populations and the immediate profit that overfishing can provide to economic groups or the convenience of disposing of chemical residues or plastic directly in the water, the dispute is simply unequal. With weakened democratic processes at the national level and their virtual inexistence in the global sphere, we have come to witness the vast destruction of the environment and the exacerbated exploitation of populations. As democracy is dismantled, the ability to represent the general interests is being appropriated by the corporate groups themselves. In the name of reducing the State, they generate an increasingly invasive and controlling machine.

Another powerful mechanism is corporate gigantism in alliance with clusters of interests. The "arch of fire" that destroys the Amazonian rainforest provides a clear illustration. Powerful corporations are in the business of hardwood trade. These precious woods did not have to be planted, and exploitation becomes strong. After this fine merchandise is removed from the forest, another interest group, in the soy business, finances fires and trunk removal. This will open the way for some excellent harvests, satisfying the equally powerful grain sector. Having lost their forest cover and after over-exploitation by grain monocultures, the soils become fragile, opening the way for extensive livestock production; it's the powerful meat industry's turn. The converging interests of the wood, grain, and meat industries lead to the powerful domination of the national political scenario, with enough representation in Congress to weaken the legislation that protects forests and riparian zones, and approve the use of toxic chemicals.

Both the concepts of diffuse interest and power clusters help to size up the broader power concentration, which bypasses the control of the democratic systems of representation or even takes them over. We come back to the title of Otávio Ianni's study, *A política mudou de lugar* (Politics has moved to a different place). The question we must face is quite clear: will we, the *homo sapiens* that we are, with our ability to rationally analyze the dynamics and take measures, be able to revert the tendencies?

V –

THE LIMITS OF RATIONALITY: AFTER ALL, WHAT ARE WE?

Even if immense opportunities arise with the knowledge society, the immaterial economy, and global connectivity, in truth, it will all depend on our ability to make use of them. Regardless of the analyses about social classes, labor organizations or political parties, and regardless of the possibility we have of creating a democratic media, it is urgent today to understand more realistically what we are as people, as human beings. Am I moving beyond economics, taking some steps outside of what can be called my field of expertise? Certainly, and it is what economists have always done when, for instance, they established the entire edifice of economic theory, inherited from the previous centuries, on a huge psychological simplification. For the equations to make sense, it was necessary to imagine that humans rationally maximized advantages, being thus scientifically predictable beings. This made it possible to present economics as a science. This is utter nonsense. We have developed sophisticated scientific constructions based on a false premise. A recent wave of studies demonstrates that this is, as Michael Hudson puts it, *junk economics*.[20]

Naturally, we like to consider ourselves as rational beings, superior to animals with their instincts, and capable of rationally determining our future. This is clearly a case of wishful thinking, an illusion about our nature. It is gratifying to feel superior. Indeed, we are always in search of rational justifications for our actions or beliefs, absurd as they may be. The concept of rationalization summarizes quite well this precarious construction around options with very little intrinsic rationality.

The Nazis were perfecting a superior race, the Ku-Klux-Klan executioners were cleaning the country and protecting white maidens, the Latin-American dictatorships were protecting us from communism, the invasion

---

[20] Robert Skydelsky presents a devastating common-sense analysis in *What's Wrong with Economics?* Yale University Press, 2020.

of Iraq was protecting us all from weapons of mass destruction, the Brazilian coup was meant to reestablish the economic balance and combat corruption, Lula was arrested because he is a thief, and so on. Today, rationalizations are created on an industrial scale by companies specializing in political marketing, with the support of think tanks, sectors of the academic world, and, of course, an immense communication machine connected to platforms, which directs personalized information. Reality has been substituted by narratives. Any similarity with rational thought is a mere coincidence, or an *a posteriori* construction.

This dimension of our behavior is essential to understand our enormous difficulty in creating a functional society. One thing is analyzing power dynamics and structural difficulties: taking into account, for example, that the economy has become global while governments are national, or that technologies advance much faster than our ability to create instruments of governance. However, understanding to what point our irrationality as human beings makes it difficult to create a functional society is an entirely different thing. Have you ever stopped to think about the absurdity of the wars and massacres that century after century we endure, for ridiculous reasons? Clearly, our definition of *homo sapiens* is quite exaggerated. How does the actual human work?

The primate inside us

Avoiding the term barbaric is impossible when, in an era of enormous global wealth, we let 6 million children die each year for lack of access to food or clean water: we know where they are, we have the resources and we are perfectly aware it costs much less to counteract the situation than to deal with the consequences. Nonetheless, we do little or nothing. The global commotion with the rescue of 12 children from caverns in Thailand shows we are capable of solidarity. But it is impossible to ignore that every day, 15 thousand children die due to lack of food. Solving this would cost very little and would save children that would later become productive individuals. Is it the spectacle that moves people? How can we have 820 million malnourished people, a figure that once more is rising, when we not only produce more than we need but waste enormous amounts of it? How can we watch, impotent, as families drown in the Mediterranean and the environment is destructed? Or, do nothing as corporations and governments, equipped with the latest technologies and managed by individuals with higher education and vast cultural education, regularly commit fraud? We can gather the most fantastic technological advances to reach our goals, but the goals themselves are deeply rooted in the murky waters of instinct, prejudice, and hatred, despite our frequent outbursts of generosity.

Volkswagen's elaborate software for defrauding particle emission verification in their vehicles is impressive in technical terms. The program was developed by people who are perfectly aware that 7 million people die annually due to the generated pollution, especially children and elderly people. The fraud was set up together with large advertising campaigns, inciting people to choose these cars for their environmental friendliness. What kind of person manipulates information about medications or pesticides and sleeps at night, at home with their families? Commercial media obviously take us for fools, but our ability to believe in completely foolish arguments is amazing, considering we are also capable of achieving wonderfully creative feats. When Jessé de Souza talks about the stupidity of our elites, he is not referring to the lack of intelligence, but to the imbecilic way they use it. And frankly, when it comes to the fairy tales told to us, our gullibility is quite impressive.

It seems we have been forgetful of our origins. We are primates. Smart primates, of course, but one thing is having intelligence, and the other is choosing how we use it. And here we go to the depths of emotions, of instinct, of our primitive roots. Not necessarily to evil, obviously. We have powerful instincts that lead us to collaborate, to maintain love relations, to defend justice, but to do evil deeds, also. And there we have wars, greediness, extreme violence, the destruction of the environment, and generalized frauds. How can *homo sapiens* fall so low?

The thing is, we are not divided between good and bad people, we have a broad potential for both. Curiously, analyzing primates provides us with a disturbing mirror to our behavior. Born in 1948 in the Netherlands, de Waal was a prominent researcher of primate behavior. His research was strongly focused on ethical behavior. After many books on primates, he wrote one about "the primate inside us", creating an interesting parallel, sometimes amusing and sometimes depressing, between ourselves and other primates. The truth is, a group separated itself from the apes millions of years ago, going on an independent evolutionary path that resulted in gorillas, orangutans, chimpanzees, bonobos, and, naturally, in the one writing and the one reading this text. This group shares some common behavior.

An interesting example is the existence of scapegoats in chimpanzee communities. There may be a fight among the more powerful in the group hierarchy, but the one who lost or who was humiliated up there will rapidly take it out on some poor weaker or younger element, and get their revenge. Someone will pay the price, even if they have nothing to do with the affair. De Waal's comparison is excellent. We recommend that Fiesp read him.[21]

> For modern man, scapegoating refers to inappropriate demonization, vilification, accusation, and persecution. Humanity's most horrific scapegoating was the Holocaust, but letting off steam at the expense of others covers a far wider range of behavior, including witch-hunting in the Middle Ages, vandalism by the fans of losing sports teams, and spousal abuse after conflicts at work. And the mainstays of this behavior – the innocence of the victim and a violent release of tensions – are strikingly similar among humans and other animals. (…) We surround this process with symbolism and pick victims based on things like skin color, religion, or a foreign accent. We also take care never to admit to the sham that scapegoating actually is. In this regard, we're more sophisticated than other animals. (169)

Sound familiar? *Homo sapiens...*

"No matter", writes de Waal, "the lack of any proven connection to 9/11, the bombing of Bagdad was a great tension release for the American people greeted by cheerleading media and flag-waving in the streets. Immediately following this catharsis, though, doubts began to surface. Eighteen months later, polls indicated that the majority of Americans considered the war a mistake. (…) It's depressing to see that we share this tendency – which creates so many innocent victims – with rats, monkeys, and apes. It's a deeply ingrained tactic to keep stress at bay at the expense of fairness and justice" (171).

But primates also owe their success and survival to a set of collaborative practices and impressive demonstrations of solidarity and compassion. The author provides several examples, which we can also find in famous videos showing primates saving children, or sharing food. Mothers also form solidarity organizations to protect their young and group members. These primates' social organization, their ability to form solidarity or rivaling groups, their feelings of outrage with injustices – seen for example in animals that refuse food when other members of the group didn't receive

[21] At the time of the impeachment of Dilma Roussef, Fiesp, the Federation of Industries of the State of São Paulo, launched a campaign against the rise in tax rates. The campaign supporting Dilma's impeachment, which also encouraged people to protest in the streets, was called *Não vou pagar o pato* – literally, I won't pay the duck. The popular saying indicates an unwillingness to pay for someone else's mistakes.

any – show that the separation of good and evil is deeply rooted in our genes. De Waal strongly criticizes the distortion of Darwinism, which justifies so many "inhuman" (!) behaviors claiming they are natural, the "survival of the fittest".

> Darwin himself, however, was anything but a Social Darwinist. On the contrary, he believed there was room for kindness in both human nature and in the natural world. We urgently need this kindness, because the question facing a growing world population is not so much whether or not we can handle crowding, but if we will be fair and just in the distribution of resources. Will we go for all-out competition or will we do the *humane* thing? Our close relatives can teach us some important lessons here. They show us that compassion is not a recent weakness going against the grain of nature but a formidable power that is much a part of who and what we are as the competitive tendencies it seeks to overcome. (176)

One of de Waal's important distinctions is between moral principles and cultural norms.

> For example, one of my first culture shocks when I moved to the United States was hearing that a woman had been arrested for breastfeeding in a shopping mall. It puzzled me that this could be seen as offensive. My local newspaper described her arrest in moral terms, something having to do with public decency. But since natural maternal behavior cannot conceivably hurt anybody, it was no more than a norm violation. By the age of two, children distinguish between moral principles ('do not steal') and cultural norms ('no pajamas at school'). They realize that breaking some rules harms others, but breaking other rules just violates expectations. The latter kind of rules are culturally variable. In Europe, no one blinks an eye at naked breasts, which can be seen at every beach, but if I were to say I had a gun at home, everyone would be terribly upset and wonder what had become of me. One culture fears guns more than breasts, while another fears breasts more than guns. Conventions are often surrounded with the solemn language of morality, but in fact they have little to do with it. (202)

The division between "us" and "the others" has an enormous influence on moral behavior. We can find much solidarity and even sacrifices among members of a primate community, and "animal" (!) behavior of the same intensity in confrontations with other communities. There is a famous idea according to which human beings would only show general solidarity if the planet were invaded by aliens. De Waal shows to what extent morality and solidarity have deep roots in the terror and hatred that the "other" inspires. This consideration helps us understand our complexity and the coexistence of contradictory feelings. Good and evil, rational and irrational, are deeply connected.

> In developing universal human rights – that must apply even to our enemies, as intended by the Geneva Convention – or debating the ethics of animal use, we apply a system that for within-group reasons outside the group, even outside the species. (...) Our best hope for success is based on the moral emotions, because emotions are disobedient. In principle, empathy can override every rule about how to treat others. When Oskar Schindler kept Jews out of concentration camps during World War II, for example, he was under clear orders by his society on how to treat these people, yet his feelings interfered. (…) We rely more on what we feel than what we think when solving moral dilemmas. (224)

It is not, therefore, that we must be more rational, but that we must use reason for a more humane society.

As a whole, reading de Waal, it is extremely instructive to see this to-and-fro between humans and other primates' behaviors, especially the bonobos, who prefer love over war. We have a strong tendency to cover up the most rotten aspects of our behavior through moralizing discourses and even through erroneous interpretations of Darwin, as we saw. But the fact is that the roots of behavior are deeply connected to our feelings, and in this aspect the parallel with primate behavior is fruitful. Being able to let go of our worse dimensions in the name of heightened ethical motivations produces immense satisfaction. We know how to do good, we know how gratifying it is, but it is so easy to go down the path of hatred. And the feeling is so powerful!

Motivations and justifications

To understand our reality, we must rationally measure the influence of irrationality. We must understand how often people use rational arguments to justify absurd behavior. Barbarism always finds "good reasons". In the words of Jonathan Haidt, "we lie, cheat, and justify it so well we start to honestly believe we are honest" (82). I can't avoid thinking of those people cloaked in the Brazilian flag, during the stage that preceded the 2016 coup, protesting in front of FIESP in *Paulista* Avenue. This was not due to a lack of intelligence, but to enormous ignorance and an immense ability of self-deception.

Self-righteousness expresses a person's deep conviction that they are dominating others from the height of their ethical superiority. This usually leads to highly moralistic and intolerant behavior. And we frequently see violent actions being justified by morally elevated finalities. All forms of barbarism protect themselves with noble arguments. This provides an excuse for unleashing hatred, that pleasant feeling of hating for good reason. The March of the Family with God for Liberty[22] was a historical mark of hypocrisy in the defense of privilege. More marches and demonstrations followed. Hypocrisy has long legs. Invading other countries is usually meant to protect a defenseless population, dictatorships are meant to save democracy, attacks on divergent sexual options are based on the feelings of superiority of people who think they use concave and convex parts properly, or according to God's demands.

Haidt, in his book *The Righteous Mind*, distinguishes this type of mentality from the regular "moral" person's mind by presenting a relatively simple problem: American society divides itself, in a relatively balanced manner, between Democrats and Republicans. Each side firmly believes they are in the superior sphere in the ethical battle, and considers the adversary hypocritical and deceitful, in short, devoid of any morality. Immorality lies with the other. However, on both sides, there are intelligent, sensitive, and at times brilliant people – and they are deeply divided. In the name of ethics, hatred rules.

The subject is not new, of course. Written in the 1940s, Gunnar Myrdal's *American Dilemma* is, to this day, an influential book in the United States, and earned him a Nobel prize. It is one of the finest analyses, not of the United States but of the good standard American. The author asks himself how is it possible that the same individual who is fully committed to his town's religious service, who has a deep conviction of the importance of freedom and human rights, will also persecute black people? Myrdal warns that he disallows any use of his analysis for cheap anti-Americanism. His objective is not to defend or attack, but to understand. But he concludes that "the negro problem" in the United States "is a white problem". The analysis could naturally be extended beyond the American mentality.

Haidt's field of work is moral psychology. He studies precisely how, in psychological terms, our value constructions, particularly what we qualify as political values, are interrelated. What actual basis do we have for considering our actions to be morally correct? What are the mechanisms that transform reason into a mere rationalization of underlying emotions?

---

[22] In Portuguese, *Marcha da Família com Deus pela Liberdade*. A series of demonstrations of the conservative sectors of society against the communist threat, that took place in Brazil in 1964, weeks before the military coup.

Laws exist, for sure, but they define what is legal and were frequently created to make legal what is morally indefensible. Tax havens make it possible for corporations to pay very few taxes. This is not an option for a small company. It's not illegal to declare your headquarters are located in a tax haven, and avoiding paying taxes in the country where your company operates, while your employees pay taxes regularly since the taxes are deducted from their payroll. Is it enough to be within the law to be ethical? When Snowden revealed the extent of the privacy invasion and the invasive use of tracking technologies by the NSA, he committed an illegal act, according to American justice (although there is controversy). But he did this, at his own risk, for ethical reasons. Those who fought against slavery were arrested and condemned. Mandela spent 30 years of his life in prison for fighting against a legal but medieval regime. Republicans say Snowden is a traitor, just as the Mafia considers a traitor to be any person who does not sympathize with the group, even if it is because this person doesn't want to commit crimes. Ethics can be quite flexible.

Is there a trustworthy perspective, an absolute value? Durkheim wrote that "everything which is a source of solidarity is moral, everything that forces man to regulate his conduct through something other than the striving of his ego". In his study, Haidt searches for the "mechanisms that contribute to suppress or regulate self-interest and make cooperative societies possible" (270). Paulo Freire, who was a simple person, but not a simpleton, summarized the problem by saying that he wanted "a less wicked society". What are the psychological mechanisms that make social groups capable of justifying in ethical terms what is clearly harmful to others and advantageous to themselves? Haidt calls this "motivated reasoning" (159).

Haidt goes to the heart of rationalizations. His view is that to us it is more important to *seem* good than to actually *be* good.

> We lie, cheat, and bend ethical rules often when we think we can get away with; and then we use our moral reasoning to manage our reputations and justify ourselves with others. We believe in our *a posteriori* reasoning so deeply that end-up self-righteously convinced of our own virtue. We are so good at it that we manage to fool even ourselves. (190, xv)

To Haidt, reasoning essentially serves the purpose of justifying what has already been decided by other intuitive mechanisms. "It is the first principle: intuition comes first, strategic reasoning second" (xiv). The result is a confirmational reasoning, not one meant to analyze and understand: "what chance is there that people will think in an open-minded, exploratory way when self-interest, social identity, and strong emotions make them want or even need to reach a preordained conclusion?" (81).

One of Haidt's greatest contributions is making it possible to understand a bit better our sea of hatred and political identifications. He provides a detailed description, based on research, of the diversity of human motivations. He works with a "moral matrix" with six foundations that underlie our attitudes of solidarity or indignation, approval or hatred.

The first is Care. This makes us avoid harming others and strive to reduce suffering. It is inside us all. When we see a puppy being mistreated, we become outraged, even if we don't like dogs. It is a powerful engine, one that requires those who massacre or torture others to "dehumanize" their victims, making them a pretense object: a terrorist, a communist, a wrongdoer, a gay, a whore, anything that lowers a person's status, making it possible to treat them inhumanely. The middle-class big boy who sets fire to a tramp feels he is, even more, a "person", that he is "above". The tramp is not a person, he is a tramp. "Get a job, you bum."

Liberty is another foundation of values, one that brings with it the corresponding rejection of oppression. Naturally, for many, liberty also means the liberty to oppress. To do so, it is also important to reduce the human dimension of the oppressed. The legal scholars of the past solved their dilemma by saying that "the liberty to have and hunt slaves" was justified on the basis that "negroes have no souls". Any value must create a curtain of hypocrisy so it can be violated. In the name of liberty, both in the United States and in Brazil, restrictions on personal firearm possession were repelled, although we know that owners are the first victims. However, we do acknowledge the aspiration of freedom as a fundamental value that guides our ethical choices.

The third foundation of values is what we call Fairness. Every weekend, millions of Brazilians are outraged when the referee shows a yellow card to a player for misconduct, but fails to do the same when the player is from the other team. If the player deserved the card, the outrage sprouts from unfair treatment. This is a perfectly valid ethical criterion and the reason why millions are outraged by the unequal treatment of the justice system, which is represented by a balance, a symbol of impartiality. This is a deeply rooted feeling.

The fourth foundation is Loyalty, which makes us strive to adopt the values of our group and consider a traitor to be whoever fails to adopt them. The *esprit de corps* is widely used in the military forces. This is how the military swears, with tranquility, that their colleagues did not torture or rape because they feel loyal to their companions. This loyalty is even above ethical considerations on a committed crime and produces a pleasant feeling of heroic belonging to a group. A famous Al Pacino movie, *Scent of a Woman*, is about this subject: a young university student who realized his colleagues were involved in a minor misdemeanor refuses to denounce them, even if this puts in peril his future in the university. His suffering is present throughout the entire film, precisely because the character is a deeply ethical young man.

The fifth set of values is founded on Authority, which leads us to consider ethical whatever the leaders decide, and label subversive whoever rebels against these decisions. This *a priori* identification with authority is a slippery slope, especially because it leads us to do anything on the grounds that we were told to. Here, Hannah Arendt's excellent text helps us understand that the issue goes beyond convicting whoever hides behind the authority argument. It is important to understand how evil is trivialized, and the type of hatred that many people have against those who strip them of what they consider to be legitimate hatred. We will return to this shortly. But try to tell someone with right-wing views that the Brazilian Federal Supreme Court's ruling was prejudiced: they will be shocked; we are stripping them of the pleasure of hatred. One must be blind to ignore the distortions, but seeing them requires the use of reason, the ability to objectively contest. There is a well-known experiment in which university students were called to give strangers an electric shock, at the request of faculty members wearing doctor coats who would tell them the experiment had scientific purposes. Most students did not have to be asked twice.

The last foundation of ethical reasons described by Haidt is Sanctity. This group is connected to tradition or religious reasons. They lead us to condemn to hell those with diverging world views (297). We have several examples here. A good reading on the subject is the Inquisition's instruction manual, which taught, for example, that women who were suspected of witchcraft or possession should be tortured naked because this would weaken them, with their back turned to the torturers, because their expressions of pain and despair, a work of the devil himself, could be so strong that the inquisitor's heart might be softened. All of this was done in the name of Jesus, of charity, of loving one's neighbors. The practice of mutilating little girls' vaginas still affects millions of children. What was done or still is done in the name of God or tradition is heinous. We are in the 21st century.

Comparing the views of numerous interviewed participants in the entire political spectrum, from the left to the most conservative, Haidt concludes there is a clear distinction regarding the elements of the matrix that matter the most to them. Those in the left-wing spectrum gave much more importance to the first three foundations: avoiding harm to others, reducing suffering, and providing care; fighting against oppression and towards liberty; and guaranteeing clear rules to the game and equal treatment, what we call social justice. Inversely, conservatives most valued the last foundations, focusing their views on loyalty to a group (see the KKK, for example) and to authority in the form of obedience; and respect to sacred, largely religious values, in which the sacred dimension is a mixture of political and religious elements, like the Nazi's *Gott Mit Uns* together with the *swastika*. The fact that there were millions of fanatics in Germany, a country that did not have low levels of either education or culture, is meaningful. It is not a question of education, but institutions, and political culture. Barbarism is not determined by diplomas.

Haidt, a self-professed liberal in the American sense, corresponding to a progressive among us, has an interesting conclusion. The right wing uses arguments and feelings that resonate deep within people, because they are strongly anchored in emotions, in feelings related to group belonging, cohesion, the flag, religiosity, authority, and obedience. This is known as the gut feeling. I usually say these are thoughts that migrate to the liver, messages that echo more emotionally than rationally, especially the narratives that provide a legitimate *façade* to our hatred. The American right wing, for example, has always selected a demon – foreign, naturally – to justify anything: Khadafi, Saddam Hussein, Osama Bin Laden, even Fidel Castro, and now terrorism in general. In Brazil, we have the excellent example of *Veja* magazine, which thrives on raising hatred against the demons that explain all misfortunes. It doesn't solve anything, but it works. The persecution of Dilma, Lula's absurd arrest, the hatred against the Brazilian Worker's Party, are all behaviors that dismiss deep thought. This is hatred in search of a justification to manifest.

Explaining the drama of hunger (the harm foundation) and the statistics of childhood mortality is an appeal to rationality in the first place. It does not have the same mobilizing effect of arguments with an emotional background, like the one that says immigrants will steal your job. The appeal to emotions gives the right wing the advantage of a simplified discourse, one that reaches the liver more readily than the mind, like

Collor's *marajás*[23] (maharajas) flag, or Jânio Quadros' *vassourinha.*[24] The hatred of corruption is a traditional tool to mobilize the masses, with the obvious advantage that it seems naturally legitimate. The problem is that the fight against corruption is rationally done through transparency, which present-day technologies can achieve. This is very different from fighting corruption for political reasons, channeling hatred instead of actually changing procedures.

Haidt searches for a more balanced world. The motivations most valued by the right wing will not disappear. The essential aspect of the book is that it lets us better understand the emotional roots of reason, the ease with which pseudo-reasons and fanaticism are created. It helps us, for instance, to understand how a campaign is built against the presence of Cuban doctors in regions where our own doctors don't want to go, an unassailable project, from a humanistic point of view. Several reasons are presented, which barely cover the ideological hatred that actually motivates the campaign. Hatred, as a mass phenomenon, is contagious. Rationally explaining a project is much less contagious.

Haidt is particularly worried about a type of power without any moral obligations: the power of corporations.

> So, if the past is any guide, corporations will grow ever more powerful as they evolve, and as they change the legal and political systems of their host countries to become ever more hospitable. The only force left on Earth that can stand up to the largest corporations are national governments, some of which still maintain the power to tax, regulate, and divide corporations into smaller pieces when they get too powerful. (297)

We are reminded of Milton Friedman, from the Chicago school, who says that companies, like walls, have no moral sentiments. The *Greed is Good* quote, which expresses the mentality of Wall Street, is also appropriate here. It seems that a large part of the world is devoid of any ethics. The movie *The Wolf of Wall Street* naturally comes to mind. The real-life character said in interviews that the movie did not exaggerate anything. We reach the

---

[23] TN. *Caça aos marajás*, or Hunt for the Maharajas, was the name given to Fernando Collor's fight against public servants with excessively high salaries. At the time, he was the governor of the state of Alagoas. Collor later became the president of Brazil and was impeached.

[24] TN. *Varre varre vassourinha*, meaning "sweep, sweep, little broom", was the president Jânio Quadros' campaign jingle, meaning sweeping away corruption.

common denominator that guarantees the general absolution: "everyone does it, we didn't do anything that all of Wall Street doesn't do".

Here, we have the issue of the dilution of responsibilities in the legal entities. Joseph Stiglitz, a former chief economist of the World Bank, a recipient of the "Nobel of Economics", and unsuspected of leftism, summarized the issue in a speech in the UN about human rights and corporations:

> But unfortunately, the collective action that is central to corporations undermines individual responsibility. It has been repeatedly noted how none of those in charge of the big banks that brought the world's economy to the brink of ruin have been held accountable for their misdeeds. How can it be that no one is responsible? Especially when there have been misdeeds of the magnitude of those that have occurred in recent years?

When we are a mass, and everyone acts in the same way, what happens when a young man is lynched in the slum, or when there are gang rapes or massacres during a war? In a gigantic corporation, where everything is diluted, ethics becomes so diluted it disappears.

No one likes to think of themselves as a person without ethics. And our defenses are strong. I cannot fail to mention the brilliant 1861 text by John Stuart Mill about the subjection of women in Great Britain at the time. They were reduced to little decorative clowns and forbidden from having any adult participation in society and any role in the creation of their destinies. In seeing how hard it was to penetrate the prejudiced mind, Mill writes:

> So long as an opinion is strongly rooted in the feelings, it gains rather than loses in stability by having a preponderating weight of argument against it. For if it were accepted as a result of argument, the refutation of the argument might shake the solidity of the conviction; but when it rests solely on sentiment, the worse it fares in argumentative contest, the more persuaded its adherents are that their feeling must have some deeper ground, which the arguments do not reach; and while the sentiment remains, it is always throwing up fresh intrenchments of argument to repair any breach made in the old.

The liver, or gut, is powerful, and many prefer it over the brain. Politics in particular navigates here.

Haidt is not patting the backs of the left or right wing. Rather, he is suggesting we should try to better understand how political groups, identifications with certain flags, and occasional fanaticisms are formed, as well as how we primarily divide society into good and bad. Manichaeism is dangerous. When we realize the same person can perform both horrendous and heroic acts, our attention turns to what really matters: creating institutions that help to value our more positive dimensions. In Haidt's words, creating "the contexts and social systems that enable people to think and act well" (92).

The triviality of evil

Cruelty plays a crucial role here. How can humans allow themselves to so easily become bestial? It would be quite easy to reduce the problem to social aberrations, to the presence of certain mentally ill individuals, without whom society would be decent, "normal". It is likewise easy to reduce Nazism to the character who created it. How much longer will we consider the incessant wars throughout human history, the massacres, rapes, and torture that have always characterized human relations and that are today generalized, as abnormal periods? We have increasingly sophisticated technologies, prodigious advances that are the result of our intelligence, but we still have the ever-present bestiality.

The nature of evil is a central issue for Hannah Arendt. When she covered the trial of Adolf Eichmann in Israel, for the New Yorker, she was expecting to see a Nazi monster, a killer beast. What she saw, and she was the only one to see this, was the triviality of evil. She saw a bureaucrat worried about following orders, for whom orders replaced independent thought or any thought beyond duly fulfilling orders. His were technical concerns, distant from ethics. Triviality makes life much easier; following orders is simple. Servitude is towards those above and brutality towards those below: two behaviors in one. The analysis of the trial, published in the New Yorker, caused outrage, especially among the Jewish community, as if Hannah Arendt were absolving the defendant, excusing the monstrosity.

The triviality of evil, however, is central. My father was tortured during the Second World War, in the South of France. He was not Jewish. So much has been said about the Jews in the Holocaust, a tragedy whose tragic dimension no one will deny, that people forget this war made 60 million victims, out of which 6 million were Jews. The persecution reached the left as a whole, Unionists or activists of any nationality, besides gypsies, homosexuals, and anyone who seemed different. The fact is that torture, extreme violence against another human being, has marked me since childhood. But as a child, I didn't know that I would suffer such violence myself. Were those who tortured my father monsters? There might have been a particularly perverse torturer, who took pleasure from suffering, but in general, these were men like any others. Situations of generalized violence and trivialized suffering give way to the worst there is in many of us.

Why is this so important? Because monstrosity is not in the person, it's in the system. Some systems trivialize the evil that is latent in us. This means that the actual meaningful solutions to protect us from totalitarianism, from the right of a group in power to decide over the life and suffering of others, lie in the creation of legal processes and democratic institutions and cultures. In this way, we may live in peace. The threat and the greater evil are not in the existence of mentally ill individuals who make fun of other people's suffering – for instance, skinheads who burn a poor man sleeping on the streets just for kicks – but in the systemic violence exerted by common people.

Among those who interrogated me in the DOPS[25] of São Paulo, was a graduate policeman who had studied in *Colégio Loyola*, in Belo Horizonte, as did I, in the 1950s. It was a Jesuit school, where they taught us to "love one another". I saw a normal man, who explained to me that if he obtained more information, he would be promoted. He even explained the possible promotion levels at the time. Apparently, he wanted to make progress in life. Another one I met was a violent former *jagunço*[26] in the Northeast. To him, torture was clearly something trivial, something he surely saw in the farmlands of his childhood. Were they monsters? They did monstrous things, but the true monstrosity was the ease with which violence was practiced, and the ease with which superior institutions provide support for it.

A torturer of the OBAN gave me a big file with copies of the testimonies of my companions who had been tortured before me. The request was simple: since he didn't want to go through all the trouble, he asked me to check the others' testimonies, and do mine confirming that what was written was the truth, even in the case of nonsense, or lies. He explained that if I wrote a testimony, repeating everything they thought they knew, this would please the *coronels* on the floor above, who read the testimonies (the *coronels*

---

[25] TN. DOPS: The Department of Political and Social Order was an institution that existed during the Brazilian military dictatorship. This was one of the centers where political prisoners were tortured.

[26] TN. *Jagunço*: an armed and violent person who is usually the bodyguard of farmers in the Northeast and may also be an outlaw. The term is an important part of Brazilian history.

avoided getting their hands dirty). In this way, they would see everything was confirmed, even if the stories were absurd. He added that if there were discrepancies, they would have to bring back the prisoners who were already in Tiradentes prison and interrogate them once more until everything was checked. He wanted to save himself the work. He was not German. It was system bureaucracy. In the concentration camps, IBM managed the selection and classification of prisoners, at the time with punched card machines. In the documentary *The Corporation*, IBM clarifies that they were only providing technical assistance.

The evil is not in the torturers, it is in the men with clean hands who manage a system that leads regular men to do things such as torture. The entire pyramid goes from the man who gets his hands dirty to someone like Rumsfeld, who sends a note to the American army in Iraq, requiring the interrogations to be *harsher*, that is, more violent. Hannah Arendt was not excusing torturers, she was pointing out the actual dimension of the problem, which was much worse. Understanding the systemic dimension of the distortions has nothing to do with sparing the criminals who accepted the carrying out or ordering of monstrosities to be done. Hannah Arendt entirely and openly approved of the later hanging of Eichmann. I am convinced that those who ordered, organized, and managed torture and directly tortured people should be judged and condemned. But the fact that I hate torturers does not justify me becoming ignorant. The fight I want to fight, the one that gives results, is for a system in which torture is impracticable.

The movie's second powerful argument comes from the hysterical reactions of Jews because Hannah Arendt did not consider Eichmann a monster. Here, the issue is as serious as the first. She was stripping the masses of the immense compensating pleasure resulting from accumulated hatred, the immense catharsis of seeing the culprit hanged. People had, and still have, the right to this hatred. It is not about delegitimizing the reaction to imposed suffering. The fact is that, by removing the monstrous nature from the executioner, Hannah Arendt was taking away the pleasure of hatred, disturbing the counterbalance that hatred represents to those who were victims of it. The feeling is comprehensible but dangerous. It is widely used in politics, with terrible results. Hatred can, according to the objectives, be a fertile land for those who wish to manipulate it. And there are quite a few candidates.

When I was in exile in Algeria, during the military dictatorship, I met Ali Zamoum, an important combatant in the fight for the country's independence.

He was tortured and condemned to the death penalty by the French and later saved by independence. Friends involved in the security of the new system found one of his torturers on a farm in the countryside. They took Ali to the farm, where he found a common idiot, scared to death in a corner. What would he do? Torture a torturer? He left him there to be locked up and judged, to the general disappointment. I asked Ali one day, how did victims of torture cope with mental disorders? In his opinion, those who best found balance were those who, after independence, kept fighting. Not against the French anymore, but for the country's reconstruction, because the continuity of the fight did not erase but conferred meaning to the suffering they had endured.

In Orwell's *1984*, the employees were regularly reunited for a session of collective hatred. An image would appear on the screen of the man that should be hated, and they would all feel transported and dominated by irrationality at the sight of Goldstein. It was a general catharsis. Collectively hating is catching. We would be blind if we did not notice the use of the same procedures today, in media spectacles, and of so many leaders. The appeal to the animal inside us works well. Covering oneself with a flag is only a disguise for bestiality.

Hannah Arendt's text indicates a greater evil: the systems that lead regular men to monstrous actions. This was widely misunderstood. The fact that educated, intelligent men could not grasp the argument is in itself significant and socially powerful. As Jonathan Haidt says, to justify irrational attitudes, rational, or rationalizing arguments are created. Hannah Arendt was supposedly against the Jews and had betrayed her people, she had dated a professor who became a Nazi. Arguments were plentiful, as long as the hatred was preserved, and with it the pleasure of its legitimacy.

This issue must be highlighted. Hating the system and fighting against it require a rational thought process. Instead, it is emotionally much more satisfying to balance out all the emotional hardship that results from suffering by concentrating all the emotional load in personalized hate. In the hysterical reactions and flagrant distortions of intelligent people concerning what Hannah Arendt had said, we see the search for emotional balance. Don't mess with our hatred. The large economic groups that opened the way for Hitler, like Krupp, or the companies that automated the management of the concentration camps, like IBM, send thanks.

The movie is a mirror that forces us to look into the present through the perspective of the past. Americans feel they are perfectly justified in maintaining a broad torture system – always off American soil since this would cause certain legal discomforts. Israel created, through Mossad and related institutions, sophisticated torture centers. They are researching electronic torture systems that surpass in inflicted pain everything invented up to now. Young Americans in Iraq filmed on their cell phones the torture they practiced in Abu Ghraib. These are healthy young men and women, well educated in schools, who even have fun with what they do. In the later interviews, there were in truth many of them who denounced the barbarism or even refused to practice it. But they were the minority.[27]

The third argument in the movie, central to Hannah Arendt's views, is the dehumanization of the object of violence. Torturing a similar human being shocks inherited or learned values. Therefore, it is essential to remove the similarity. It is not a person who thinks, cries, loves, or suffers, it is a "Jew", a "communist", an "element", in the jargon of the Brazilian police; to the Ku Klux Klan, it is a negro; at the international level today, the terrorist; and in television shows, the "bandit". People have fun watching persecutions. Are they human beings? It is essential that they cease to be individuals and persons, and become a category instead. One hundred prisoners were suffocated in a cell? Well, they were "bandits".

Sebastian Haffner, a law student in Germany in 1930, wrote a book at the time, entitled *Defying Hitler: a memoir*. The manuscript was abandoned and recently recovered and published by his son. The book shows how a student from a simple family adheres little by little to the Nazi party, simply by the influence of friends, the media, and the context, repeating the messages along with the masses. In the review I wrote about the book, in 2002, I noted that what must be frightening in totalitarianism, in ideological fanaticism, is not the sick torturer, but the normal people who are pulled towards a pathological social dynamic, seeing it as a normal path. In the Germany of the time, 50% of the physicians adhered to the Nazi party. The problem was not Hitler, but the ease with which normal or even highly educated people supported and followed him, instead of placing him in a mental facility. The next political fanaticism won't wear a moustache or boots, nor will it shout *Heil* like the skinheads. The new character will wear a suit and tie and be in

---

[27] Better than any comments, is seeing the movie Ghosts of Abu Ghraib, available on YouTube at
http://www.youtube.com/watch?v=_TpWQj0MjvI&feature=youtube_gdata_player. This is about a network of death squads and torture centers in Iraq, see the BBC's research at http://www.theguardian.com/world/2013/mar/06/pentagon-iraqi-torture-centres-link?INTCMP=SRCH.

multimedia. And will for sure try to impose totalitarianism, but in the name of democracy, or even of human rights. Will we, existing people and communities, 7.8 billion people endowed with questionable rationality, be able to rescue the path of the common good?

Years ago, a student asked me what I thought would become of the human being, if the disaster we witnessed should worsen, or if there was hope, if Rousseau's view of the good man being misdirected by social dynamics had any sense. I go along the lines of the great jurist that was Sobral Pinto: institutions are fundamental and respect for the law is what saves us. That is, we must analyze in different circumstances, especially in the scope of different institutions, how the same populations can show civilized and bestial behaviors. We can remember the Nordic countries that were once Vikings, Germans who were once Nazis, Belgians who once murdered millions in Congo; and at the same time the immense progress of overcoming slavery, feudalism, and colonialism. I am not speaking of a distant past.

Fighting for civilized coexistence is done through the construction of solid rules of the game. They must be fair. They cannot systematically privilege a minority like the rules we have today. And there is a time for everything. The struggles of the Americans for getting rid of slavery, of so many countries for getting rid of colonialism, of South Americans for getting rid of dictatorships, were not only legitimate but necessary. Barbarism subsists; South African apartheid coexisted with the latest technological advances. It still exists in Palestine in this strange mixture between technical modernity and human tragedy.

This present detour in our line of thought, this discussion on the collective human distortions in a study about the knowledge society and the modes of production, makes a whole lot of sense to me. The reality is that we will have to change the world with the human being that actually exists. And this human being is only partially rational. Besides, technological advances are cumulative; one scientific discovery supports the next. But the human being that is born today has basically the same DNA as Caligula or Galileo. The cruelty that children are capable of, the pathetic behavior of so many teenagers or the pathological behavior of so many adults shows that, with each new generation, we must reconstruct a civilizing cultural heritage, indicating how easy it is to fall back into barbarism. Our civilizing advances are real but extremely frail. Without a democratic culture and its corresponding institutions, and the permanent struggle to institute and defend them, the prospects may be bleak.

VI –

THE LOSS OF CONTROL: A SOCIETY IN SEARCH OF NEW PATHS

The truth is that everything has dramatically accelerated, even before the Covid-19 crisis. Social time functions in different rhythms to technology, which advances so fast they run over us; in culture, which evolves much more slowly; and in legislation, which only changes when the accumulated transformations are literally imploding the inherited legal framework. The pieces are not adjusted to one another. The American Senate calls in Zuckerberg to understand what is going on. The system's creator answers he had no idea of the implications and asks forgiveness. Billions of people are stuck in a system whose broader dynamics no one foresaw, and blindly join a risky game. We are always late concerning technological advances, trying to find, *a posteriori,* the adequate rules for the game for a reality that is always ahead of us. How should we deal with uberization, or with electronic privacy invasions, or with the trap of indebtedness and dividend extraction?

The issue of globalization is directly connected to the technological transformations that disorganize the governance of society through the mismatch in the rhythms of the diverse social spheres. Globalization is an abbreviation for the dramatic complexity of the reorganization of the territorial base of governance. What space does a national government have for decision-making when the financial system is global? Well-educated adults shout with glee in Wall Street that *Greed is Good*, and are surprised when millions of credit users lose their houses and banks like Lehman Brothers are closed. There is a patent lack of proportion between the number of resources they manage and their ignorance regarding these resources' impact. Movies like *Inside Job* and *Capital*, among others, show either dramatically or amusingly the system's irresponsibility and chaotic dimensions. For the 820 million starving people or the millions of children who die of hunger each year, there is nothing amusing in this irresponsible chaos.

We have 21st-century technologies and production systems with a culture, institutions, and laws made for the last century. We have national governments for a largely globalized economy. In other words, it is a dilemma that would have interested Marx; we have a superstructure created to regulate the bourgeois society of the industrial era, and an economic base that has already migrated to the digital sphere. People are now realizing that the formally declared opinion of three private risk evaluation companies is vital for the survival of governments and their economic policy: Fitch, Moody's and Standard & Poor. Does this dismiss the citizens' opinion? The Economist called the three companies an irresponsible oligopoly. To whom do these companies, which define the destinies of our governments, belong?

The lack of adjustment is systemic. The global erosion of governance has disastrous impacts; we need only look at the surrealist governments we have, starting with Trump's. We are undeniably destroying the planet, the very grounds for our survival, and we do this for the benefit of the already classical 1% richest, who have the particularity of being, in the majority, unproductive or even harmful. In Brazil, after having approved the minimum rules of good sense in the 1988 Constitution, we began facing the revolt of an oligarchy that considers their indecent privileges are not being sufficiently contemplated. Instead of messing with the privileges, we mess with the Constitution. It is also said that the interests of the wealthy do not fit into the polls. For the oligarchy of the rich, there is no hesitation between their interests and democracy, even if they also suffer a setback with conflict and recession. Rationality has limited space in our brains when it comes to politics.

Joseph Stiglitz is a subversive character today, when he writes a treaty about the obvious, saying we need to change the rules of the game: his *Rewriting the Rules*, which we've seen earlier, is remarkable. In it, he calls for shared prosperity for the system to function again. Lester Brown's *Plan B 4.0* calls attention to the environmental tragedy we created and urges us to turn to a plan B, precisely because the plan A we live in, the anything-goes of the "free market" and "neoliberalism", is disastrous. There are countless examples of initiatives like *The Next System* in the USA, the *New Economics Foundation* in Great Britain, *Alternatives Economiques* in France, the *Green New Deal* and so many others across the world. Proposals like that of Bernie Sanders, calling for more decent wages and a more democratic society seem today like simple common sense for so many people who understand a little about economic policies. And the sustainable development goals, the SDGs, clearly mark the shift in the indispensable guidelines for our balance, with all the frailty of agreements established on much goodwill and very few resources.

The movement that today brings us a new wave of analyses is a welcome one. The truth is that what we call the market, in the traditional sense, with diverse companies striving to satisfy customers and competition mechanisms, has become marginal. The corporate giants and the oligopoly mechanisms have taken over. We find them in all global platforms, in the commodity traders, the big media, banks, pension funds, health insurance plans, installment plans, insurance companies, telecommunications, the pharmaceutical industry, the pesticide industry, and many other segments that are now financialized. They aren't controlled by the consumer (market competition) or by governments (regulation systems). They are still called "markets", but this is clearly a legitimacy loan, a deception. And the individuals responsible are called CEOs, when they do politics day and night.

A lot was written, and many experiences happened around the "free market" and "state planning", as opposite sides that organized society's development. What we have today does not permit either the balancing mechanism of free competition, restricted to only a few sectors, or the rationalizing ability of economic and social planning. My conviction is that the path for the governance of the system, in broad terms, requires the evolution into mixed systems, diversified according to the sector. Our societies are too complex for an administration based on simplifying ideologies, from one side or the other. I discussed the complex articulation of regulation mechanisms in another work, *O pão nosso de cada dia (Our daily bread)*, about the diversification of productive processes. Marjorie Kelly extensively discusses the transformations in the concept of property, indicating new paths along the lines of inclusive property. Elinor Ostrom provides us with excellent analyses about the relations of property in the field of common goods. China now formally adopts several interconnected subsystems of property.

The future is not very predictable. From a given number of variables that intercross in chaotic manners, we can doubtless fight for forms of governance that may guarantee a systemic redirection of our paths, in a context with at least some individual liberty. But the result will be far from a rational construction, or something predictable. In other words, the future is uncertain. What we do know is that with the current tendency, with environmental tragedies, exploding inequality rates and financial and technological resources serving all but the necessary purposes, we are heading towards what was rightly named a slow-motion catastrophe.

Regarding our initial hypothesis, with the new technical and social relations, and new forms of power and surplus appropriation, will a new systemic balance arise, another mode of production? The new forms of domination will no longer necessarily characterize a capitalist mode of production, and the alternative is not necessarily only socialism. As the current tendencies progress, the emerging feeling is that we are rapidly evolving into a surveillance society. In this, the social and environmental tragedies will be explained as necessary by an increasingly unbalanced power which will be more oppressive due to this imbalance. This pessimistic view is related to what we have observed and does not reduce the need to fight for forms of development that bring dignity to all, are sustainable in the long run, and capable of transforming threats into opportunities. As Ignacy Sachs likes to say, a pessimist is a well-informed optimist.

Democratic socialism, in its root sense of social and democratic appropriation of our development processes, is more palpable than ever. Continuing to call what we experience as capitalism can be slippery: to many, capitalism is responsible for the world's growing wealth and essentially has a positive value. To others, it symbolizes exploitation. The system we face today has lost the dimension of enriching societies and aggravates exploitation. It has basically become a parasitic system, each time requiring more truculence to maintain itself.

It is becoming harder to deny that, after decades of tending to the animal we knew, industrial capitalism – qualifying it as the 3rd or 4th industrial revolution, adding names to it like global or financial capitalism, or other complements according to the shape it assumed –, today we must consider in systemic terms what other animal is emerging. The basic economic unit is not the factory anymore, but the platform; the product is increasingly immaterial; the work relations are increasingly diversified and fragmented and wage work is steadily decreasing; the form of extraction of surplus-value is increasingly centered on financial mechanisms of exploitation; the free market, as the central regulating mechanism of capitalism, is limited to marginal segments; the property of the means of production has radically lost importance and other forms of control are arising, especially through the financial system; the power over populations is exerted more and more through media control mechanisms, algorithms, and privacy invasion; governmental space, within national boundaries, seems to be losing the ability to guarantee functional governance; the legal systems are being taken over and we are losing the rules of the game that gave us some assurance.

On the other hand, individuals can now connect with the world from their pockets; and, naturally, the main factor of production, knowledge, has an unlimited potential of access. We have already gone through this argument; I bring it back because of its central importance in the restructuration of society since the economic analysis has radically changed and is no longer based on the allocation of scarce resources. In the era of virtual money and connectivity, financial systems themselves create an opportunity for radical de-intermediation. The more modern technologies, such as the Brazilian social welfare program *Bolsa Família* and the microcredit systems, make it possible to radically solve our world's biggest scandal, hunger and childhood mortality, with minimal costs in comparison to the waste of resources and their merely speculative use. And we can redistribute work and reorganize working hours, with more people working and more people having time to live. We live in an era where opportunities are massively wasted or underused. And decision-making processes can be radically democratized, in the direction of horizontal networks.

A central question appears concerning the destiny of class struggles. The labor world is fragmented in highly diversified sectors and subsectors, making it hard to create interconnections. The industrial workforce is a minority, even in highly industrialized countries. In the USA, they represent approximately 10% of the active population. With the fragmentation of the labor world, unions and parties have also become weaker as tools for organized political action. What has happened to the "dominant class" today, the rich and unproductive 1%? Their lack of productivity and the setback they represent to progress generate an immense weakness in comparison to last century's bourgeois forms of exploitation. The former capitalists at least produced shoes, paid wages, albeit low ones, and paid taxes. They could claim that more money to the bourgeoisie meant more investments and progress. Not anymore. Today's capitalism does not make but hinders progress. It is systemically dysfunctional. Authoritarianism, in the absence of legitimacy, has become essential to keep a system that is progressively losing functionality. The deterioration of the democratic spaces worldwide finds an explanation here.

This authoritarianism sustains itself especially in the new and robust power cyst which we have vastly underestimated: the "shock-troopers" of the ultra-rich: the economists, lawyers, managers, information specialists who occupy the top of the hierarchy in the decision-making processes and who maintain the distorted system we have today. They control the machine and receive millionaire wages and bonuses. Thomas Piketty presents them in a central role in the imbalances of income and wealth. But the main aspect is the power they have inside the corporate giants in terms of guiding the use of our resources. They control key positions, take turns between the administrative councils of the corporations and public functions (what we call the revolving door) and, in the age of the new technologies and of management by algorithms, concentrate a massive amount of power in their hands. Flexibility is not expected from this new upper middle class. Nor should we think these privileged people will think twice before extending the reach of oppressive systems of social control. Think of the power of the young executive from Serasa-Experian to place us among the class of "in default" individuals because we find ourselves in financial difficulties. This person has the power to deprive us of a series of rights. At the same time, the banks that practice usury don't even have a regulating institution (or only a fictitious ones, like the central banks or the BIS – Bank for International Settlements).

Our studies have, in general, been limited to assessing income levels and defining a middle class and an upper middle class. More importantly, however, we should understand their roles in the gears of power. We must understand the joined forces that this technocracy represents, with its key roles in corporations, governments, legal systems, the media, and in the think-tanks that create "narratives". They form today a system with different types of class organizations. But they are connected and feel united because of the convergence of interests. Class struggles have moved to a different place and technocracy has come to play an essential role in the immaterial-based society, in total convergence with the big rentist fortunes: they are, also, among the most interested in financial profit. The small bourgeoisie, analyzed by Marx, the small-scale proprietors of the means of production, differs profoundly from this massive power machine represented today by technocracy, in the scope of an economy centered on controlling information and financial flows.

The world dominated by corporations is no longer controlled by market competition, which to some extent balanced the game, and even less by the political system that should guarantee a counterbalance through regulation. We have the truculence of the private sphere without the checks of the public sphere. The corporate world is vigorous, global, uncontrolled, and armed with new technologies that provide the means for a radically amplified extraction of the social surplus. These technologies also assure much more penetrative forms of controlling people's consciousness.

Corporations flex their muscles and aim directly at the main dish: maximizing profit, right now. This is high technology at the service of short-term appropriation, with little regard for the economic, social, and environmental disaster produced.

To a numbed world, the fairy tale of merit and efficiency is offered, of wealthy people being the ones responsible for boosting the economy. And since the feeling of indignation demands culprits and a place to deposit hatred, the dramas are being presented as the State's fault. Nothing that a cut in corporate tax rates and more privatizations won't solve. The irony is that today the accused public administrations are controlled by corporations. Ultimately, of course, the unconvinced can have the truncheon.

The animal is clearly not the same. It has become a chaotic, uncoordinated animal during its metamorphosis, but it is doubtless a different thing. We stand somewhat fascinated and somewhat fearful, and observe a process whose dynamics we clearly don't fully grasp. The benefit of considering another system, or mode of production, is that we can think of the necessary new rules for the game, instead of struggling to make the world function according to the old framework, with improvised equipment. The superstructures need to be redeveloped, given the profound changes in the productive base of society. Are we allowed to dream a little?

For example, in this era of the dominance of unproductive financial rentism and the accumulation of gigantic speculative fortunes, we need to make disclosure, or transparency, compulsory. We have to adapt the tributary system aiming to reorient resources towards productive activities. If we add a small fee for financial transactions, we would produce at the same time resources for productive investments and transparency of the flows. Both the Tobin fee on transactions and the tax over financial capital that Piketty describes already show us a way. In this case, we would be shifting tax incidence.

In this era, in which the main factor of production is immaterial and can be disseminated without additional costs, the concept of the private property of means of production, the legal base of capitalism, must be shifted towards remunerating creators but without hindering access and reproduction by third parties. A variety of studies have shown that patent and copyright systems hinder more than they foment innovation. It is a matter of adjusting the notion of property to social productivity. The works of Lawrence Lessig, Jeremy Rifkin, Don Tapscott, and many others show the way.

As new technologies are rapidly inserted in the new age and substitute the workforce, we must build the corresponding new rules to the game. We need a new concept of the social contract, combining the progressive reduction of working hours and a fairer redistribution of the right to employment/work, as Guy Aznar proposes. Several countries are already moving in this direction. A fairer distribution of access to work and income is then a possibility and with it a new generation of activities connected to the discretionary use of free time. This includes time with family and community, time for culture, sports, and other activities. The idea that having more technologies at our disposal and, thus, more productive capacity, is a threat to us is nonsense. The real threat is the delay in adjusting the forms of organization of our time and income. A better life is within our reach.

To face the explosive global inequality, we must bring together a basic universal income and access to social policies such as health, education, and security, among others. In this way, we will be able to manage the disturbance and uncertainty that accompany the present transition from the factory era to the knowledge society. In Brazil, 38% of the active population is in the informal sector, grabbing whatever they can find to survive. The figure rises to nearly 50% for the Latin-American average and 70% in Africa. Expecting people to keep waiting for a job is not realistic. People in desperate situations react desperately. Common sense dictates we should avoid the aggravating social convulsions. In economic terms, the simple observation is that the costs of guaranteeing the basic needs for everyone are much lower than the costs of dealing with the consequences. Will we build more walls along borders? The world now has more than enough resources to assure the minimal conditions of survival with dignity to all. The billionaire's accumulation shows wit, not wisdom.

With a largely global economy, we can no longer manage ourselves through a miscellany of the different constitutions of 195 member-states of the UN, while the major decisions are being taken by giant corporations that obey no constitution at all. The basic rules of international relations must be reconstituted since we are planet Earth and there is no substitute planet. We must ensure a minimum of global coherence. In the globalized world, the absence or weakness of global rules, barely compensated by the 2030 Agenda, means the deadline for our destruction will hit our children. The destructive impact of global corporations takes place precisely where global governance is absent. How much longer will we passively watch our future being destroyed? The stupidity of the big corporations' management lies in the fact that its members benefit from maximizing results in the short-term, and their advisors too, in the form of bonuses earned. The sum of the individuals' selfishness does not result in altruism or minimally responsible decisions. All the large banks contributed to the 2008 crisis. Don't they understand finance?

Considering, in particular, the abyss of inequality between rich and poor countries, ensuring a new North-South pact is urgent now. We may consider the model of the Global New Deal, proposed by the UNCTAD and systematized in different documents, including the impressively predictive Brandt report, *North-South*. Instead of protecting their borders with walls and electrified fences to keep out the poor, the rich of the world could use some economic reasoning: the needs of the poorer countries are an immense fertile land for expanding investments, representing potential new markets and an underused workforce. Once again, policies for investing in poor countries should not be seen by the rich as a form of draining their wealth, but as an opportunity for those countries to leave stagnation. Financial transaction taxation and a wealth tax may serve to co-sponsor an initiative of this size. There will evidently be no solution without activating the more than 20 trillion dollars from speculation sitting in tax havens. Great Britain has taken the first steps in this direction by demanding that British Overseas Territories at least advise to whom the capitals belong. This is how far we've gone: only the very first timid steps.

The world quickly advances towards generalized urbanization. This opens an enormous space for communities themselves to take control of development policies, city by city, because each one of them knows their needs better than any minister, and will be able to take better care of the productive application of resources. The structural vectors of the economy are no longer manufacturing and agriculture, but rather health, sports, education, culture, information, leisure, security, and others – the social policies. Corporations have been taking over these policies, generating excessive costs and unequal access conditions. This appropriation dynamics must be substituted by universal and free access. Management must be at the level of people's lives, at the city level, in the scope of decentralized and participative policies. As we saw, this cuts costs instead of pushing them up. It is not through vouchers like Ronald Reagan's that access will be democratized but through local development policies, in the framework of the effective empowerment of communities. The examples of the Nordic countries (see *Viking Economics*, by George Lakey), of China (*China's Economy*, by Arthur Kroeber), Germany (*The Public Bank Solution*, by Ellen Brown), and others show the immense potential of rationalizing management through the decentralization of the decision power and its corresponding resources.

In the intangible-based era, where most of our activities surround the magnetic signals of our computers or cell phones, we must review the concept of privacy that is present in the constitutions. Today, it is illegal to open a person's private correspondence, but the full-scale invasion of our messages, pictures, or files is a generalized practice. It's used to elect surreal politicians and obtain commercial advantages, if not for different types of bullying and persecution. According to the new rules of the game, the right to privacy must have a central role. Our lives are currently wide open, while the activities of legal entities, the corporations, are protected. The opposite must happen. Because of their social impact, and because they are legal entities, entrepreneurial activities must be made transparent, while the private lives of individuals must be protected.

Is it possible to put forward proposals in this direction? It all depends, naturally, on the relations of power, which in turn largely depend on how far the population is aware that they are being fooled, and also that they have immense opportunities arising with the knowledge society. As has been said, let us not underestimate the power of ideas. It has, in fact, transformed the world.

VII –

THEN AND NOW: THE MAJOR TRENDS OF SYSTEMIC CHANGE

To facilitate the view of the whole, we organized this table of changes, a type of "then and now" that may here help to recognize the broader spectrum. We will provide a paragraph commenting on each axis of change. According to our hypothesis, taken together these axes generate a new system. The arguments are repetitions of the previous chapters, but the goal here is precisely to make the overview easier.

20th Century	21st Century
Machines	Knowledge
Factories	Platforms
Tangibles	Intangibles
Proportional costs	Zero marginal cost
Expansion of productive capacity	Restricted access
Purchase and ownership	Right to access and use
Sales profits	Support profits
Informative marketing	Individualized manipulation
National space	Global space
Traditional exchange of products/raw materials	Technological dependency
Global liberalism	New protectionism
Salary remuneration	Piece-rate remuneration
Expansion of employment	Elitism and marginalization
Low salaries	High debts
Financial subsidies	Financial speculation
Money printed by governments	Digital money emitted by banks
Profit	Dividends
Government for citizenship	Government for corporations

1 – From machines to knowledge: This is the most profound transformation of all since it impacts all other transformations. Power, in the broad sense of the main dynamics of economic and social organization, has shifted from land controllers, in the feudal era, to machine controllers in the industrial capitalism era, to knowledge controllers today. This new power also controls the information systems corresponding to the new knowledge, including modern forms of money, which are now magnetic signals.

2 – From the factory to the digital platform: We still have General Motors and other factories, but the factory workforce in an industrial country like the United States now represents less than 10% of the total workforce. Today we have a wide variety of systems that manage magnetic signals: GAFAM in the West, BAT in China, all the financial systems like Wall Street and City, and the banks that have systemic importance. None of them is interested in serving productive chains. On the contrary, they control and exploit them. In a way, the castle represented the feudal power, the factory, the strength of capitalism, and the digital platform, which banks have also become, the new economic dynamics.

3 – From tangible to intangible: While the production of physical goods is becoming increasingly technology-dense, the whole process, from financing to commercialization and distribution, besides control and management, is becoming essentially intangible. Intangible assets, in turn, can be managed through magnetic signals, software, algorithms, and artificial intelligence. Because of this, they function on another economic logic; they become infinitely replicable and communicable. André Gorz uses the concept of the "immaterial".

4 – From proportional costs to zero marginal cost: Producing more units of clothing requires more raw materials, in an amount proportional to the volume produced. In Jeremy Rifkin's excellent formulation, we are entering the era of the zero marginal cost: once the initial costs of research are covered, its replication and dissemination require no additional input. A book, song, or idea online may be disseminated with no additional costs. This generates today a widespread confusion between the concept of private property of the last century and the modern forms of appropriation of non-rival goods. More people reading my book online does not bring me any additional costs.

5 – From increasing production to restricting access: Henry Ford understood perfectly well that to increase his profit, he had to increase the scale of production, reducing the cost per unit (economies of scale) and reaching more customers. When I use Microsoft Word, I generate no additional cost to the company, but access to the software is restricted by law; because access is blocked, people pay for it. It is a 'monopoly of demand' because I am forced to use whatever everyone else is using. There is no viable competition. This encompasses technology and ideas in general and leads to the absurd expansion of patents, copyrights, royalties, and other forms of making money without more effort: additional money without additional work. This is also true for common goods like water in regions where it is scarce, like privatized beaches or parks. Air and water have an enormous use-value, but the means for increasing the exchange-value is by restricting access.

6 – From purchase to the right to access: In our daily lives, a growing portion of our income is no longer being spent on products that we purchase and become ours, concluding a commercial transaction. We spend it, rather, for obtaining the right to minimally decent TV programming, access to health services, an internet connection, mobile telephony, complementary security systems, and so on. As consumers, we are tied to a "plan", including fidelity requirements and fines if we decide to exercise our right to prefer the competitor. But here, a wide spectrum of opportunities equally emerges: instead of the ownership of a car, for instance, I can prefer access to one, as in the case of Paris' public cars. It is cheaper for everyone. In Brazil, we have barely implemented shared bicycles.

7 – From product sales to support services: Eric Raymond, in *The Cathedral and the Bazaar*, notes this well: processes connected to knowledge are interactive. Buying software is only a small part of it. Most important now are the support services, maintenance, and updates. "If (as is generally accepted) over 75% of a typical software project's life cycle costs will be in maintenance and debugging and extensions, then the common price policy of charging a high fixed purchase price and relatively low or zero support fees is bound to lead to results that serve all parties poorly" (120 and ss.). The logic of commercialization changes: we buy a product cheaply, but what they actually sell us, in the long-term, is the need to recur to support services, owned by the same group. Haven't you ever replaced the drum in your printer?

8 – From informative marketing to individualized manipulation: Privacy invasion has, besides fomenting consumption, become the instrument for customized and personalized manipulation. Corporations and governments now have detailed information about what we read, our political interests, health conditions, illness propensities, interests, and other sectors of our life. We only discover how important this information is when an old email undermines our job search, or previous personal communication interferes in obtaining a visa, or we are charged more for life insurance because of the information the company bought about our DNA, and so on. This is, strictly speaking, a new world. Personal microchips and human microchip implants are a reality already, despite it still raising protests. It is all in our best interest, naturally, but our best interest is defined by others. Indeed, with individualized control over people and their behavior at the most intimate levels, the world's power relations radically change. *Big Brother is watching you*, this time for real, and obviously not only referring to the State.

9 – From the national to the global sphere: The economic system, especially in its financial dimension and in the immaterial sectors (communication, information, etc.), has come to work in the global sphere, giving rise to expressions like *space is dead*, or books like *The world is flat*. The book I search for on Amazon may be anywhere in the world. A query may find the information I seek in any document, in any language, in any institution. But the regulation system – the laws that aim to bar usury, fiscal evasion, antibiotic use on our food and others – varies throughout the 195 countries of the world. That is, the economy functions largely beyond the reach of laws. The loss of governance and of the capacity to implement policies at the governmental level tends to spread. People are starting to ask themselves what is the sense of voting. We have a global economy, but no global government, and very few coordination systems.

10 – From the traditional unequal trade to technological dependency: We are used to seeing the dominant countries supply finished products and machines in exchange for raw materials. This is still largely true, but the level has shifted. Today, the production processes may be transferred to countries where the workforce is cheaper. However, access to technologies, brand usage, and similar immaterial products is restricted. Denying the right to the autonomous production of medications, for example, is a global scandal, causing immense suffering and death. Ha-Joon Chang, in *Kicking Away the Ladder*, shows how all these countries that have always copied everything until they became dominant now attack any attempt to make access easier. Several authors and institutions have risen against this new cycle of dependence that increases inequality. The broadening of patents and copyrights is actually a new form of protectionism, adapted to the knowledge economy, as are the customs tariffs on physical goods, widely denounced by globalization supporters.

11 – From global liberalism to new protectionism: In economic terms, in the information era, the transaction costs of the ownership systems – in time, money, messy bureaucracy, loss of collaborative potential, sterilization of the network effect – are generally higher than the benefits. The profits of groups that control access to knowledge and culture are, although substantial, minimal relative to the losses (this is called loss of profit, or ceasing profits) that result from the halt in creative processes and the restrictions on the use of the innovations in the world. Considering the number of major issues whose solution now depends on the democratization of knowledge, placing tolls everywhere to maximize profit has become irresponsible. We refer here to the knowledge needed to reduce inequality, the clean technology needed to reduce climate impact, the authorization that is necessary for the decentralized production of medication to face the humanitarian tragedies, among other significant problems. Open access is economically more viable and productive and results in more and not less creative activity. The developed world, which controls 97% of innovations (Chang), halts the outer circulation of technologies that the world needs so much and creates walls to protect itself from the poverty it produces.

12 – From salary remuneration to piece-rate remuneration: The creative contribution of innovative ideas does not depend on the amount of time we spend in the office. Gorz mentions a report from the Human Resources Director of Daimler-Chrysler: the contributions from the "collaborators", as he gently calls them, "will no longer be assessed by the number of hours they put in but on the basis of objectives achieved and the quality of outcomes. They are entrepreneurs" (17). Resorting to workers only when they are needed for specific tasks opens the way for outsourcing and a set of informal hiring platforms. The impacts on income levels and union organization are quite clear. Such structural changes affect the whole of labor relations.

13 – From the expansion of employment to the growth of elites and the increase in marginalization: The expansion of industrial activities provided the amplification of direct and indirect labor throughout the world. New companies meant more jobs. The process continues, no doubt, but new companies have increasingly become synonymous with fewer jobs. The United Nations created the expression "jobless growth". There have been several catastrophist predictions, but the reality is that we have reached a threshold in which the rhythm of the emergence of new activities does not compensate for the lost jobs anymore. More sophisticated labor, in terms of technology, has expanded, but the labor force that can be substituted by machines and algorithms has decreased, widening the gap between "professions" and a simple work force. Marginalization especially hits the developing world, where the dynamic is cloaked as the "informal sector", the "self-employed" and the "self-entrepreneur", but in truth, they represent the widespread loss of the means to make a living. The wall built and panic raised among the wealthy because of immigrants are pathetic, but the people living in the poor neighbourhoods of Brazilian cities face the same violent reality.

14 – From salary exploitation to the debt trap: Workers' purchasing power depends of course on wage policies. Traditional exploitation uses low wages, resulting in surplus-value. Today, however, the debts of individuals, companies, and States have produced a radically more powerful form of exploitation. In Brazil, the annual interests paid by families and especially by small- and medium-sized companies represent approximately 16% of the GDP, while part of our taxes is transferred to financial intermediaries for the public debt service at the rate of 6% to 8%, depending on the year. This is more than 20% of the GDP serving as a mechanism for exploitation. When people pay 100% interest on installment plans, they are having their purchasing power reduced by half, and the need to pay in time will be transformed into an extortion mechanism. The mechanisms are comprehensively described in our *The Era of Unproductive Capital*. Didactic videos are also available at dowbor.org. The process has become global. In Brazil, it is only more gruesome.

15 – From financial subsidies to financial speculation: In Brazil, banks insist on calling everything investment, whether you are building a school or making financial investments. I can earn money from financial investment yields, but it will be a wealth transference. I did not produce anything. A part of the wealth produced by society simply changed hands. In the era of financialization, securities have yielded 7% to 9% in the last decades, while the production of goods and services, the world GDP, grew only 2% to 2.5% per year. The majority of the population lacks the financial resources to make financial investments, but the rich invest a lot and make a profit from high interest rates and dividends without having to invest in production. The speculative mechanism has become the main form of wealth accumulation. Productive capital has been transformed into unproductive capital. The more you invest, the more you earn. This generates the present-day absurdity of the 1% richest families having more wealth than the other 99%. This radical transformation in the forms of exploitation explains both rising levels of inequality and sluggish economic growth, despite the copious technological advances. It also explains China's economic growth, since their financial system is controlled and directed to productive investments.

16 – From money printed by governments to digital money emitted by banks: private printing of money is a criminal offense, but a bank creating money out of nothing is the dominant way of expanding credit, and generating debt. Lehman Brothers emitted debt to the level of 31 times what it had in deposits; an impressive leverage made easy when money is just a digital sign on computers. The loss of control over money emission by banks leads to permanent irresponsible activities by private groups big enough to make sure they will always have access to Quantitative Easing and support ultimately coming from our taxes. Control over international speculative transactions in digital money has become fictitious. More than 90% of global money is digital.

17 – From profit to dividends: The increase in financial investments instead of productive investments shifts social surplus appropriation from "profit" to "dividends", the latter resulting from different speculative processes. Even in corporations that effectively produce goods and services, at the top of the pyramid, a bond is formed between the executives, who now earn approximately 300 times what the average workers make, and the shareholders who appoint them. The result is wage stagnation and increased exploitation. Company CEOs are paid largely in company shares. This promotes solidarity towards external shareholders. The capitalist entrepreneur is no longer in charge of the corporation; the CEOs are, and they depend on the financial controllers, the absentee owners, in Marjorie Kelly's formulation. In Brazil, the distributed dividends are not subject to income taxation, even if they are in the millions. In the exploitation system, a huge step has been added.

18 – From a government for citizens to a government for corporations: Power relations have changed, in the sense that any elected government must respond more to the requirements of the so-called markets than keep their commitment to citizenship. We've seen earlier Wolfgang Streeck's clear systematization of the dilemma between the State for the people and the State for the market: the time of democratic capitalism is fading away. Donald Trump's administration, for instance, reduced taxes on corporations, hindered environmental and social policies, and placed Goldman Sachs executives in his economic team. This illustrates the shift in power relations and the depth of transformations. The admittance of bankers to the Central Bank's board of directors and to the Ministry of the Economy in Brazil reflects the same tendency. We are not in the lobby era anymore. These actors now directly exercise power. The 2018 presidential elections only aggravated the distortion. The pandemic support money basically went to banks, and stagnated there.

This set of transformations generates a system with a different logic. Another productive base, other forms of commercialization, other remuneration and exploitation dynamics, other bases for power and control over populations. It is especially not a question anymore of free market competition, with the traditional invisible hand. The system is now based on the interconnected power of corporations, ruled by the heavy hand of the financial system, and it is taking over the State itself. It is time to review our frames of reference.

Our interest in focusing more on the future being outlined than on the past that becomes distorted as we move makes it easier for us to understand the systemic dimensions of a new mode of production based on financialization, information, knowledge, and connectivity, which have, as a whole, been called the intangibles or the immaterial. Just as we had a land-based age, and another age based on industrial activity, today a new age is rapidly emerging, based on a different logic. This age has the potential to both increase oppression and exploitation and lead to collaboration, openness and liberation. Limiting ourselves to trying to resist the distortions is not enough. We must direct our research towards the logic and potentials of the future, in this digital revolution.

The common denominator we are searching for is the liberation of the positive potentials of the knowledge age, with open and democratic access to knowledge, and de-intermediation of financial systems. We must channel our new abilities to face the two widening catastrophes that threaten our civilization: environmental destruction and explosive inequality. We have the means and the ends; what we need is to create the policies. Looking at our planet in this new millennium, we tend to consider that we are entering the age of knowledge with *homo sapiens* technologies, but primate policies. Ours is not an economic but a civilization challenge.

BIBLIOGRAPHY

Alperovitz, Gar, & Lew Daly. *Unjust Deserts: How the Rich Are Taking Over Our Common Inheritance.* The New Press, New York, 2008.

Angell, Marcia. *The truth about the drug companies, how they deceive us and what to do about it.* Random House, 2005 (*A verdade sobre os laboratórios farmacêuticos – Ed. Record, 2007.* https://dowbor.org/2007/08/a-verdade-sobre-os-laboratorios-farmaceuticos.html/).

Archibugi, Daniele, David Held & Martin Kohler. *Re-imagining Political Community: Studies in Cosmopolitan Democracy.* Stanford University Press, California, 1998.

Bauman, Zygmunt. *Capitalismo Parasitário.* Zahar, Rio de Janeiro, 2010.

Campello, Tereza. *Faces da desigualdade no Brasil.* FLACSO Brasil, 2017. http://dowbor.org/2017/12/tereza-campello-faces-da-desigualdade-no-brasil-um-olhar-sobre-os-que-ficam-para-tras-flacso-brasil-2017-80p.html/.

Chomsky, Noam. *Manufacturing Consent.* Pantheon, 2002.

Dauvergne, Peter. *Will Big Business Destroy our Planet?* Polity, Cambridge, 2018.

Dembinski, Paul, Alain Schoenenberger. *Financial markets*. Eco'Diagnostic, Geneva, 1993

Dowbor, Ladislau. *Hannah Arendt: além do filme*. 2013. http://dowbor.org/2013/08/hannah-arendt-alem-do-filme-agosto-2013-3p.html/.

Dowbor, Ladislau. *The Age of Unproductive Capital: new Architectures of Power.* Cambridge Scholars, UK, 2019. https://dowbor.org/2019/06/l-dowbor-the-age-of-unproductive-capital-new-architectures-of-power-cambridge-scholars-uk-2019.html/.

Gerald Epstein and Juan Antonio Montecino. *Overcharged:the high cost of high finance. T*he Roosevelt Institute, July 2016 http://rooseveltinstitute.org/overcharged-high-cost-high-finance/

Friedrich Ebert Stiftung. *Digitalização e o futuro do trabalho – Resumo do estudo "Trabalho 4.0"* do Ministério do Trabalho da Alemanha, outubro 2017. www.fes.org.br.

Gorz, André. *O imaterial: conhecimento, valor e capital.* Anna Blume, São Paulo, 2003.

Guardian. 13 Jan., 2018. *Tencent*. https://www.theguardian.com/business/2018/jan/13/tencent-the-500bn-chinese-tech-firm-you-may-never-have-heard-of.

Haffner, Sebastian. *Defying Hitler*. St. Martin's Press, New York, 2003 [1939]. http://dowbor.org/2003/08/defying-hitler-a-memoir.html/.

Haidt, Jonathan. *The Righteous Mind: Why Good People Are Divided by Politics and Religion*. Pantheon Books, New York, 2012, 420 pp. ISBN 978-0-307-37790-6.

Harvey, David. *A loucura da razão econômica: Marx e o capital no século XXI*. Boitempo, São Paulo, 2018.

Haskel, Jonathan and Stian Westlake. *Capitalism without Capital: the rise of the intangible economy*. Princeton University Press, Oxford, 2018.

Heaven, Douglas. How Google and Facebook Hooked us, and how to break the habit. *New Scientist*, Feb. 7, 2018.

Hazel Henderson – *Reforming Money and Banking* – Ethical Markets, NY, 2015. http://www.tikkun.org/nextgen/reforming-money-and-banking-keys-to-debt-and-jubilee

Kelly, Marjorie. *Owning our Future: the emerging ownership revolution*. Berrett-Koehler Publishers, Oakland, 2012.

Kelly, Marjorie, and Ted Howard. *The making of a democratic economy*. Berrett-Koehler, Oakland, 2019.

Lessig, Lawrence. *Remix – Making art and commerce thrive in the hybrid economy*. Penguin Press, London, 2008.

Mazzucato, Mariana. *The Value of Everything*. PublicAffairs, New York, 2018

Mill, John Stuart. *The Subjection of Women* [1861]. Dover Publications, New York, 1997.

Myrdal, Gunnar. *An American Dilemma: the negro problem and modern democracy*. 1944 – inúmeras edições, inclusive em português.

Ocampo, José Antonio. A reforma da tributação corporativa internacional: a perspectiva da ICRICT. *Nueva Sociedad*, julho de 2018. http://nuso.org/media/articles/downloads/TG2_Ocampo_EP18.pdf.

Ostrom, Elinor and Charlotte Hess. *Understanding knowledge as a commons*. Cambridge, MIT Press, Cambridge, 2007.

Oxfam. *A distância que nos une,* Oxfam, setembro 2017. http://dowbor.org/2017/09/a-distancia-que-nos-une-oxfam-brasil-setembro-de-2017-94p.html/.

Oxfam. *Uma economia para os 99%,* Oxfam, janeiro 2017. http://dowbor.org/2017/01/oxfam-uma-economia-para-os-99-2016-relatorio-10p.html/.

Oxfam. *Extreme poverty versus extreme wealth: how big is the inequality gap?* Oxfam, 2018. https://www.oxfam.org/en/even-it/5-shocking-facts-about-extreme-global-inequality-and-how-even-it-davos.

Rifkin, Jeremy. *The empathic civilization: the race to global consciousness in a world in crisis*. Penguin, New York, 2009.

Rifkin, Jeremy. *The Zero Marginal Cost Society: the internet of things, the collaborative commons, and the eclipse of capitalism*. New York, Palgrave Macmillan, 2014. Online at http://digamo.free.fr/rifkin14.pdf.

Sims, Julian, et al. *How Money Works*. Penguin Random House, London, 2017. www.dk.com.

Skidelsky, Robert. *What's Wrong with Economics*. Yale University Press, 2020.

Souza, Jessé & Rafael Valim (orgs.) *Resgatar o Brasil.* Contra Corrente, São Paulo, 2018.

Stiglitz, Joseph. 2013 UN Forum on Business and Human Rights. http://www.ohchr.org/Documents/Issues/Business/ForumSession2/Statements/JosephStiglitz.doc.

Stiglitz, Joseph. *Rewriting the rules of the American economy: an agenda for shared prosperity*. New York, London, W. W. Norton &Company, 2015, 237 pp. ISBN 978-0-393 -25405-1.
http://dowbor.org/2016/09/stiglitz-rewriting-the-rules-of-the-american-economy-an-agenda-for-shared-prosperity-new-york-london-w-w-norton-company-2015-237-p-isbn-978-0-393-25405-1.html/.

Stiglitz, Joseph, and Bruce Greenwald. *Creating a Learning Society: a new approach to growth, development and social progress.* Columbia University Press, New York, 2014.

Stout, Lynn. *The shareholder value myth: how putting shareholders first harms investors, corporations and the public*. Berrett-Kohler Publishers, San Francisco, 2012.

Sundararajan, Arun. *The sharing Economy: the end of employment and the rise of crowd-based capitalism*. Cambridge, MIT Press, 2016. ISBN 9780262034579.

Susskind, Richard, & Daniel Susskind. *The future of professions: how technology will transform the work of human experts.* Oxford University Press, Oxford, 2015.

Toussaint, Eric. *Le système dette: histoire des dettes souveraines et de leur répudiation.* Editions Les Liens qui Libèrent, Paris, 2017.

Tuchman, Barbara. *The March of Folly*. Random House, New York, 1984.

UNCTAD. *Trade and Development Report 2017: Beyond Austerity, Towards a Global New Deal*. Unctad, Geneva, 2017.

Vitali, S., J. B Glattfelder and S. Battiston. ETH, *The Network of Global Corporate Control*. http://arxiv.org/pdf/1107.5728.pdf.

Waal, Franz de. *Our inner ape: a leading primatologist explains why we are who we are.* Riverhead Books, New York, 2005.

Zuboff, Shoshana. *The Age of Surveillance Capitalism*. Public Affairs, New York, 2019.